UNTO OTHERS

Rediscovering the Golden Rule — The Lost Key to Relationships

Dave Swavely

To my wife Jill, who has lived "unto others"
more than anyone I know.

CruciformPress

"One of the most comprehensive and practical treatments I've ever seen. You won't want to miss this!"

"A practical guide, anchored in rich theology, about how to live out the Golden Rule daily in community and culture."

"Historical perspective, skillful use of Scripture, and sound doctrine act as a foundation and context."

"A breath of fresh air… just the right balance of law and gospel… as useful for evangelism as it is for edification."

"Sorely needed for the divisive, dysfunctional times in which we live."

"Confronts the confusion and cultural misgivings that have jaded the meaning of this most consequential command."

"Practical, life-altering truth… clear, doable, life-changing, relationship-changing, church-changing, and society-changing."

"Readable, positive, and interesting… historical, theological, and biblical. Ideal for group study or classroom use, with questions that conclude each chapter."

"In reading it, I have rediscovered the Golden Rule. This central teaching of Jesus rea`lly is a treasure."

"The Golden Rule is truly a key that unlocks priceless treasure and not a mere truism. I highly recommend Unto Others.*"*

"Recent biblical law studies demonstrate that **the essence and purpose of the law was to display the perfect character of God in values**. Rather than look for current applications to specific OT laws, we as twenty-first century Christians should understand and amplify the values behind the law in every aspect of our lives. **Dave Swavely's study reduces these values to one, because Jesus did.**"

> **Dave Deuel**, ThM, MPhil, PhD, Academic Dean Emeritus, The Master's Academy International and Senior Research Fellow and Policy Advisor, the International Disability Center at Joni and Friends

"In this book, Dave Swavely has explained, illustrated, and applied the truths found in a statement made by Jesus Christ as part of the greatest sermon ever preached, commonly called The Sermon on the Mount. **Dave has corrected the misunderstanding and misapplication of the statement called The Golden Rule,** clearly demonstrating its relevance and applicability to living in our present-day world."

> **Wayne Mack**, DMin, author of *A Practical Guide for Effective Biblical Counseling* and *Discipleship and the Christian Life Issues* series based on *The Pilgrim's Progress*

"You have likely heard the expression, 'It goes without saying... ' I had put the Golden Rule from Christ's Sermon on the Mount in that category. I assumed everyone knew it and understood it. Dave Swavely's book, *Unto Others*, made me realize how naive I was. In this clear and concise exposition, Dave clarifies what the Golden Rule is and what it is not, and how it reflects God's wisdom for healthy relationships. This book is **sorely needed for the divisive, dysfunctional times in which we live.**"

> **Stan Gale**, DMin, author of *Finding Forgiveness: Discovering the Healing Power of the Gospel* and *The Vine-Ripened Life: Spiritual Fruitfulness Through Abiding in Christ*

"Dave Swavely **takes us to a new place of understanding** this ancient belief and bold claim by Jesus. He explains the history, philosophy, and theology of the Golden Rule, highlighting the fact that it is so much more than just a nice thought. In fact, it is impossible to follow without the transformation of the Gospel and the power of the Holy Spirit. *Unto Others* is **insightful and motivating** for us to become more like Christ by applying the Golden Rule."

> **Elaine Griffith Petty**, MS in Bioethics, international consultant, speaker, leadership coach

"This book is **a practical guide, anchored in rich theology, about how to live out the Golden Rule daily in community and culture.** Dave explains and illustrates well the tragic and devastating effects of disconnecting this saying of Christ from gospel and theological truth. When that happens, it becomes a self-serving path to self-promotion and a self-righteous path to self-redemption. Devoid of its gospel roots, the Golden Rule becomes merely a shallow, moralistic slogan. But, when understood and practiced in the context of all Scripture, it robustly displays God's magnificent mercy and grace."

> **Bill Hill**, MM, DRS, Executive Director of Equipping Nationals Worldwide and author of *Toward a Theological Examination of The Call, Election and Evangelism: Pursuing Balance and Biblical Clarity*, and *Pastors Training Pastors: Restoring the Pauline Model*

"In *Unto Others*, Dave Swavely draws readers' attention to the importance of understanding and living by the Golden Rule. He explains well how followers of Christ not only must believe correctly (i.e., orthodoxy), but also act correctly (i.e., orthopraxy). The description of the true meaning of the Golden Rule is **one of the most comprehensive and practical treatments that I've ever seen.** This is a book that you won't want to miss!"

> **Matthew Akers**, PhD, Associate Dean of Doctoral Studies, Director of the Hispanic Institute, Mid-America Baptist Theological Seminary, author of *Equally Yoked* and *One Lord, One Faith*

"The Golden Rule and its call for agape love is a summary command, one that encapsulates other commands (Rom. 13:10). Dave Swavely picks up on this biblical priority in his book, *Unto Others*, as taught by Jesus. **The Golden Rule is truly a key that unlocks priceless treasure and not a mere truism**—when its practice is motivated by the gospel of Jesus and gratitude to God. Swavely reminds us to treat people not as they wish per se, but according to the Scriptures—an excellent clarification—and provides helpful practical steps for how to apply the Golden Rule. I highly recommend *Unto Others*."

> **Greg E. Gifford**, PhD, Associate Professor at The Master's University and author of *Heart & Habits: How to Change for Good*

"*Unto Others* revives the biblical understanding of the Golden Rule and provides practical case studies that show Christians how to apply it. It's timely, and not just because the Rule has suffered abuse even from churchgoers: We live in an age where people redefine morality, reinvent themselves, and set ungodly standards for relationships. **The book is a breath of fresh air. Swavely's exposition is solid and puts the Golden Rule in its proper context of salvation, presenting just the right balance of law and gospel** to make the book every bit as useful for evangelism as it is for edification."

> **Robert J. Burrelli Jr.**, ThM, PhD, Senior Minister, Pilgrim Reformed Bible Church

"Reading Dave Swavely's book helped me to hear Jesus' instructions to 'treat others as I would want to be treated if I was in their situation, doing what is best for them according to the principles of Scripture.' **His historical perspective, his skillful use of Scripture, and his explanation of doctrine act as a foundation and context to everything he is saying.** As a mental health professional I am always looking for practical, life-altering truth to pass on to my clients. Dave's application steps at the end of the book are very clear, practical, doable, life-changing, relationship-changing, church-changing, and society-changing, although he makes it clear that no one can consistently live the Golden Rule without true conversion and the power of the Holy Spirit. World and church history would have never been tainted with prejudice, slavery, oppression, and other forms of injustice if the Golden Rule had been practiced."

> **Vincent L. Calloway**, MSS, LCSW, CEAP, Founder of V. Calloway Counseling Associates and author of *Who's Your Daddy? I'm Your Daddy*

"Dave Swavely has done us all a favor in focusing our attention afresh on the Golden Rule. **His book at the same time is readable, positive, and interesting. It is historical, theological, and biblical.** Finally, it is very practical. It's ideal for group study or classroom use with questions that conclude each chapter. For me the book lives up to its title, for in reading it, I also have rediscovered the Golden Rule. This primary teaching of Jesus really is a treasure."

> **Curt Young**, DMin, Pastor Emeritus at Church of the Atonement and author of *The Least of These*

"Jesus was asked, 'What is the greatest commandment?' He answered, '"Love the Lord your God with all your heart and with all your soul and with all your mind." This is the first and greatest commandment. And the second is like it: "Love your neighbor as yourself."' It is amazing how many folks do not know that this is the summary of the Ten Commandments. In like manner, **people have no idea that the Golden Rule is a summary of Jesus' teaching on how to live in relationships. This work will help you understand how we lost the Golden Rule and encourage you to regain and practice it.**"

> **Howard Eyrich**, ThM, DMin, Director of Doctor of Ministry and MA Biblical Counseling Program at Birmingham Theological Seminary, author of *The Art of Aging: Preparing and Caring*, *Life Lessons from Ancient Prophets*, and *James: The Other Side of the Coin*

"As the west continues its march to a secular tune, even the most basic biblical themes and ideas are becoming increasingly foreign. The Golden Rule, taught by Jesus in the Sermon on the Mount, is one such example. Dave Swavely has written an interesting, accessible book on **a text whose meaning we misunderstand—or outright miss—to our own theological peril.** *Unto Others* reminds us that the Golden Rule is no platitude, but as Swavely perceptively notes, is **important for our salvation, spiritual growth,and service to others."**

> **Ryan Rindels, PhD,** Pastor of First Baptist Church, Sonoma,CA and author of *Andrew Fuller's Theology of Revival*

"Dave Swavely's hard work on *Unto Others* has been a blessing to me. The analysis of the loss of the Golden Rule is spot on, as well as his navigation to rediscovering the Golden Rule. I really appreciate his focus on examining your own life long before seeking to help others—this resonates with the sound doctrine of the Holy Scriptures. **Help others to rediscover the Golden Rule by encouraging the reading of this book!"**

> **Johnny Touchet,** pastor, missionary, founder of Partner 10:15 Ministries

"C.S. Lewis once remarked that a good moral teacher does not teach new morality but reminds us of the old. Dave has done just that by offering the reader a clear and convincing reminder of the foundation of the Golden Rule by confronting the confusion and cultural misgivings that have jaded the meaning of this most consequential command. In a world where substantial relationships seem impossible, Swavely reminds us of God's truth that grounds meaningful relationships and roots them deeply in the life-giving and life-sustaining Word of God. "

> **T. Dale Johnson,** Jr., PhD, Executive Director of the Association of Certified Biblical Counselors, Associate Professor of Biblical Counseling and Director of Counseling Programs at Midwestern Baptist Theological Seminary, and author of *The Church as a Culture of Care* and *The Professionalization of Pastoral Care*

Author

Dave Swavely (M. Div., The Master's Seminary) served for seven years as an assistant to Dr. John MacArthur and as a pastoral staff member at Grace Community Church in Los Angeles. Since then he has planted and pastored two churches and is currently working on a third plant, while also serving as the Advancement Officer for the international missions organization PAK7.

He coauthored *Life in the Father's House: A Member's Guide to the Local Church* (with Wayne Mack) and *From Embers to a Flame: How God Can Revitalize Your Church* (with Harry Reeder), and is the sole author of two titles that were published by P&R. He has worked as a journalist for *World* magazine and has three novels published by Macmillan. His website is *DaveSwavely.com* and he blogs at *TheWayWithWords.net*.

Dave and his wife, Jill, have been married for more than thirty years, with seven kids and three grandkids. Together they've started several innovative educational programs and housed many people in need. Dave's life journey has included many failures as well as successes, and he's learned the most from his failures.

Unto Others: Rediscovering the Golden Rule—The Lost Key to Relationships

Print / PDF ISBN: 978-1-949253-36-8
ePub ISBN: 978-1-949253-38-2
Mobipocket ISBN: 978-1-949253-37-5

Contents

Foreword
Dave Deuel

Jesus sends us into all the world to witness. He also sends us unto others in our midst to help them. Many take his Golden Rule to mean that if you want others to treat you well, then you need to treat them well first. But Jesus made a much bolder claim on our lives: treat others well regardless of whether they treat you well in return. No wonder he also commands, "Love your enemies."

Our Savior explains that the Golden Rule fulfills the law and the prophets, all the Old Testament. Recent biblical law studies demonstrate that the essence and purpose of the law was to display the perfect character of God in values. Rather than look for current applications to specific Old Testament laws, we as twenty-first century Christians should understand and amplify the values behind the law in every aspect of our lives. *Unto Others* reduces these values to one because Jesus did—love others.

In response to the Old Testament law, David models the Golden Rule. King Saul continually mistreats David, humiliating him and attempting to take his life. In response, David refuses opportunities to retaliate. The Apostle Paul does unto others. Leaders aim to harm him with false accusations undermining his good testimony. On several occasions opponents beat and stone Paul, nearly taking his life. But the apostle responds with love and kindness. He will not retaliate.

We would like others to focus on us and do for us. We are born self-interested and we live in a reciprocating world. Some say, "You scratch my back and I'll scratch yours." Jesus' message challenges the very basis of reciprocity and calls for a radical alternative: sacrifice yourself by doing unto others.

What would happen if Christians in all institutions practiced Jesus' Golden Rule? In the home, family members would draw unconditionally close in the face of mistreatment, abandonment, and divorce; in the church, people would not take offense but would generously care for others; and in society, Jesus followers would model relationships that shine bright in dark places.

In a world tragically bent on harming others before they harm you, Jesus calls you to do unto others regardless of what they do to you. This tall order comes from a God who consistently and completely does unto others with fail-safe perfection.

Dave Deuel
Academic Dean Emeritus
The Master's Academy International

Senior Research Fellow and Policy Advisor
International Disability Center, Joni and Friends

How This Book Got Started
And How I Failed: An Introduction

Imagine you've got a nickel sitting in your closet. The coin has been there for so long you don't even notice it anymore when you reach for your clothes. It lies there under the shoes and a couple of old boxes—in the dark, forgotten. What if, one day, you found out that it was worth millions of dollars?

That's what happened to the heirs of the famous coin collector, George Walton. Walton died in a car crash in 1962. His will stated that his coins were to be divided up among his relations—his sister Melva got the nickel. At the time, everyone thought it was a fake, but Melva decided to keep it nonetheless. She put it in an envelope and kept it at the back of her closet—and that's where it stayed, for thirty years. When Melva died, it was passed on to another member of the family who put it in his bedside table drawer. Another ten years passed. No one in the family thought much about the nickel, or whether the coin was worth anything.

In 2002, a group of coin collectors became obsessed with finding the lost 1913 Liberty Head Nickel. They had four nickels out of the original set of five, and they were desperate to find the fifth. They offered a one-million-dollar reward. Walton's family remembered the old nickel in the envelope and brought it in for inspection. The experts declared it to be authentic and the coin was auctioned off—fetching the extraordinary sum of $3,172,500.

What I've discovered in the Golden Rule, and want to tell you about in this book, is something like that coin—you've seen it before, but you haven't been noticing it. You've glossed over it because you aren't aware of its value.

People are fascinated with lost treasure and hidden truth. Lost treasure is a big part of the appeal of entertainment like *The Count of Monte Cristo*, *The Hobbit*,

By the late twentieth and early twenty-first century, people were no longer familiar with the Golden Rule and the saying has largely vanished from our collective consciousness.

and the Indiana Jones movies. Hidden "truth" was a big reason for the success of best-selling book, *The Da Vinci Code*. But, of course, those are just stories—whereas this book is about lost treasure and hidden truth that are *real*. Treasure and truth that can *really* change your life.

There was a time—not more than a century ago—when all Christians in America knew about the Golden Rule. Most unbelievers did too. People thought about it, talked about it, and wrote about it;

it was a prominent thread in the fabric of society. "Do unto others what you would have done to you" was displayed above school blackboards, on church banners, and in other public places.

By the late twentieth and early twenty-first century, however, people were no longer familiar with the Golden Rule and the saying has largely vanished from our collective consciousness. Since I realized this several years ago, I have enjoyed asking friends and acquaintances a series of questions to illustrate the point.

My first question is this: "Do you know what the Golden Rule is?" Some people know—but many don't, especially among younger people. I sometimes think that if I gave them multiple-choice-type answers, a lot of them would pick "A name for the Ming Dynasty in China" rather than "Jesus' summary of the biblical teaching on relationships."

Then I ask them a second question: "Is the Golden Rule actually in the Bible, or is it just an old saying along the lines of 'God helps those who help themselves'?" More than half the people I've asked think that it's just a human saying. But, in fact, the Golden Rule is straight out of the Bible.

The third question I ask is this: "Do you know where to find the Golden Rule in the Bible?" This one stumps almost everybody. In fact, I can count on one hand the number of people over the years who've got it right—and they were real Bible geeks! Actually, there are two possible answers to this question, because the Rule is quoted both in Matthew and in Luke. Here is the Golden Rule from the Gospels, in the most popular modern translation:

> So in everything, do to others what you would have them do to you, for this sums up the Law and the Prophets. (Matt 7:12, NIV)

> Do to others as you would have them do to you. (Luke 6:31, NIV)

Like me, sociologist Jeffrey Wattles also found there was a lot of confusion about the Golden Rule when he was preparing to give a series of lectures at Stanford University and write a book about the topic. This is what he said:

> A volunteer… guessed that the Golden Rule was "An eye for an eye and a tooth for a tooth." A reporter misquoted the rule: "Do to others as will be done to you." Given a correct formulation, two students debated at length with their professor that the rule meant the same as the motto "Get even." A pastor's wife doubted that the rule was biblical.[1]

So a pastor's wife doubted… but what about pastors themselves? In 1989, James Forbes preached a sermon at Riverside Church in New York titled, "Whatever Happened to the Golden Rule?" In it, he admitted that even he had trouble finding it in his Bible. And he was not only a pastor, but a professor at Union Seminary![2]

Public figures who quote the Golden Rule often *mis*quote it. For example, former President Barack Obama said in a public speech that the Golden Rule is "Love thy neighbor as thyself." Another time, he referred to it as "treating others as they would treat me."[3] And, to make sure my illustrations cover both sides of the political spectrum, I'll add that former First Lady Melania Trump quoted the Rule in a speech about the problems of cyberbullying. But she

 What happened? Why has the Golden Rule all but disappeared from evangelical thinking and discussion?

misquoted it too, saying, "Do unto others what you would have them unto you," leaving out the second *do* in the quotation. Even when people quote the verses correctly, they often don't understand what it means in the context of the rest of Scripture, or how it should be applied to our lives in a biblical way.

What happened? Why has the Golden Rule all but disappeared from evangelical thinking and discussion? This question fascinated me, so I set out on a mission to figure it out. I got more than I bargained for. Not only did I learn why the Golden Rule has been lost (see

Chapter Two), but I also came to a deeper appreciation of how important this command from the lips of Jesus is. In the pages that follow, I invite you to rediscover the Golden Rule with me, and to see how this simple maxim will help you to believe and apply the gospel in your own life. The Golden Rule is a life-changing, heavenly truth that will be worth far more to you than any earthly treasure, if you understand it rightly and practice it biblically.

Rediscovery

That "Rediscovering the Golden Rule" in the subtitle of this book has a very personal double meaning for me. I wrote the initial manuscript for this book many years ago, when I was walking with the Lord and serving him faithfully in ministry. However, by the time Cruciform Press had picked it up, my life had taken a dark turn. I had drifted away from God and my wife, and there was sin in my life which was exposed as the book was approaching publication. Thanks to God's grace, I repented of my sin and tried my best to "bear fruit in keeping with repentance," as Matthew 3:8 says. For me, this meant that, among other measures, I needed to tell my publisher that I did not feel qualified to be teaching God's Word at that time and ask that the book not be released.

Thankfully, in the years that have passed since then, God has graciously restored me to more godly patterns of walking with him and with my wife. Praise God for forgiveness and change! During that time, I've been able to reflect on how my failure to keep the Golden Rule led to my sins and their harmful effect on many people. This, in turn, led to a better book. In fact, as I returned to work on this manuscript, I felt like I was rediscovering the Golden Rule personally as much as I'm calling for its rediscovery in the church at large. And I still feel that way—the gospel truth to which the Golden Rule is meant to lead is more meaningful than ever to me, because I see just how far I've been from keeping God's law and how much I need a Savior to keep me.

one

PRICELESS

Why the Golden Rule
Is So Very Golden

Back in 2006 a book was published called *The Secret* by Rhonda Byrne, a former television producer. It raced up the bestseller lists at a record pace, notching up almost two million sales in less than six months, with almost as many accompanying DVDs. One reason for the incredible success of this book (besides being featured on the Oprah show, which must have helped!) was the marketing appeal of the title. As one book reviewer said, "It was an incredibly savvy move to call it *The Secret*. We all want to be in on a secret. But to present it as *the* secret, that was brilliant."[4]

As that article went on to say, *The Secret* was not really a secret at all. It was just a shallow promise, like the "name it and claim it" nonsense that some people still want us to believe. Those kinds of promises always lead to *you* being the focus of everything. And that will leave your life empty and meaningless, as we learn in the book of Ecclesiastes. Ironically, although this book that you're reading will sell far fewer copies than *The Secret* did, it actually contains much more of a secret to life's challenges and problems.

The Golden Rule is a real secret. Why do I say that? Because for decades it has been lost, largely hidden from common knowledge. It is also a secret in the sense that it is a hidden key that will unlock great riches in this life and the life to come. And the most distinctive thing about it…? This secret, this key, starts not with ourselves, but with a focus on *God* and *others*. As we will find, the irony is that when we focus on God and others by living by the Golden Rule, we discover that it works out much better for us. When you do unto others as you would have them do unto you, better things will be done to you.

Jesus highlights this in Matthew 7:2, where he says, "With the judgment you pronounce you will be judged, and with the measure you use it will be measured to you." We often read that verse negatively—in other words, if you judge others harshly, you'll receive back the same kind of harshness. But it can also be applied in a positive way: if you think and speak about others with fairness and kindness, you'll often be treated with the same fairness and kindness.

I won't go so far as to say that the Golden Rule is the key to everything, but I will say this: this principle is one of the greatest lost treasures anyone can ever find. It's key to our salvation, key to our sanctification, and key to our society. We'll discuss these ideas in more depth later in the book, but at this point I'll just summarize and introduce them.

The Purposes of God's Law... and the Rule

In Matthew 7:12, the first time the Golden Rule appears in the Bible, Jesus gives a reason why we should "do unto others": "for this is the Law and the Prophets." This is the only time Jesus equates a statement with "the Law and the Prophets,"[5] which is a common scriptural way of referring to the Old Testament by synecdoche (a figure of speech where part of something is used to refer to the whole thing, like "Hollywood" or "a nice set of wheels"). When Jesus says "the Law and the Prophets" just two chapters before, however, in Matt. 5:17-20, its meaning is clearly synonymous with the "commandments" of the Old Testament and therefore very similar to the way Paul uses "the law" in Romans and Galatians—to refer to the perfect standard of the Mosaic law that no one can keep (Rom. 2-7, Gal. 2-5).

In Matthew 7:12, "The Law and the Prophets" is summarized by a command (the Golden Rule), and such commands are being emphasized even when the prophets are mentioned, because one of the main tasks of the prophets was to explain and apply the law, calling Israel back to it and rebuking them for not obeying it. The prophets did talk about the promise of the gospel and its Messiah, of course (so did the law sometimes, for that matter), and we will see in subsequent chapters how the Golden Rule not only summarizes the law but also prepares us for the gospel and points us to Christ as Savior. But when you see "the Law and the Prophets" in passages like this, the meaning is basically the same as other references to "the law," because the emphasis is on the moral requirements God laid down in the Old Testament.

But there's more—the Golden Rule itself is a *new* command of Christ that also represents a perfect standard, and there were many more to come in the rest of the New Testament. So when Jesus said, "this

> *The Golden Rule not only summarizes the law but also prepares us for the gospel and points us to Christ as Savior.*

is the Law and the Prophets," we should understand it as referring to *all* the commands of God, including those in the New Testament, because they are a consistent extension and application of the ones in the Old Testament. The simplest definition of "the Law and the Prophets," therefore, is this: "the law of God," or everything God has commanded in the Bible.[6]

Why is this important to understand? Because it

shows us the importance of the Golden Rule! Since the Golden Rule "*is* the Law," it is meant to accomplish in us the same things that the law is meant to accomplish. And the law is meant to accomplish a lot! According to the Scriptures, *we cannot be saved* without it, *we cannot be sanctified* without it, and *society cannot function well* without it. Let's explore each of these ideas in more detail—they are the three uses or purposes of the law that theologians have written about throughout church history.[7]

The Golden Rule Is Key to Our Salvation
(Being a True Christian)

The first and most important purpose of the law—and also of the Golden Rule—is to show us our sin so that we might realize our need for a Savior. The apostle Paul explains this clearly in Galatians 3:19–24, where he says that the law "imprisoned everything under sin" (v. 22) and then goes on to say that the law "was our guardian until Christ came, in order that we might be justified by faith" (v. 24). When we understand the Golden Rule and how we should be living by it, we will realize why we can never be good enough to earn our way to heaven, and why we need to trust in Jesus to save us.

This makes the Golden Rule of eternal importance.

It leads us to the only all-sufficient Savior, Jesus Christ—the only one who ever perfectly lived by the Golden Rule and whose righteousness becomes ours when we believe in him. The bad news of the law (that we are sinners) leads us to the good news of the gospel (that Jesus died and rose again for us)—and the Golden Rule can lead us to a future hope of living one day on the streets of gold.

The Golden Rule Is Key to Our Sanctification
(Growing in Christ)

Once we recognize our sinfulness and need of redemption through Christ, and realize what he has done to save us, we then want to please God by obeying him. Every true Christian longs to please God—not to earn his acceptance but because we have already been accepted by God in Christ. As 1 John 4:19 says, "We love because he first loved us." So, corresponding with the second purpose of the law, the Golden Rule promotes our sanctification—it reorients our perspective away from our natural self-centeredness and towards treating others the way we would want them to treat us, namely, with the kindness and generosity that we have experienced from God in Christ (see, for example, Eph. 4:32).

The Golden Rule Is Key to Our Society

(Living Together)

The third purpose of the law, and of the Golden Rule that summarizes it, is to restrain evil and promote good in government, business, family, the arts, and other aspects of our culture. The more the Golden Rule is practiced, the more society will function as God intended it to function. It is not an overstatement to say that if we all treated others in the way we would want to be treated and did so consistently and according to a godly standard, the world would be a perfect place!

We can catch glimpses of the perfect kingdom of Christ in this world when people live out the Golden Rule in their everyday lives.

In fact, one day, the world *will be* a perfect place, when the conquering Savior Jesus Christ removes all sin and makes everything new. Then all the commands of God will be followed perfectly, including the Golden Rule, and there will be no more injustice, crime, pain, sickness, tears, etc. (Rom. 8:18–23, Rev. 21).

But even before that glorious day, we can catch glimpses of the perfect kingdom of Christ in this world when people live out the Golden Rule in their everyday lives—even if it done imperfectly. For example, one man who made this his motto in life and tried to live by it was Samuel Jones, a self-made millionaire businessman and mayor of Toledo, Ohio from 1897 to 1904. At the height of a social reform movement, this man was so associated with Jesus' saying that he was known as Golden Rule Jones. His commitment often led him to discouragement—it is so difficult to live by the Golden Rule consistently and even harder to get others to do it! But even his halting, depressing attempts to live by this teaching of Christ in business and government earned him the following eulogy at his funeral, from Cleveland Mayor, Tom Johnson:

> With a smile for a friend and a kind word for an opponent, he won his way in Toledo, in Ohio and in the nation. As my tribute to Mayor Jones I desire to say that Toledo is better; Ohio is better; the nation is better and the whole world is better for his having lived.[8]

Wouldn't it be great to hear words like that spoken about our lives? I believe we can if we rediscover the Golden Rule and live by it. In fact, we can achieve more than this man did—more lasting results, at least—if we learn to understand and apply the Golden Rule in the light of the rest of Scripture, and especially in light of the gospel of God's grace. The goal of this book is to help us to do that.

An Illustration from Jesus Himself

In Luke 10, Jesus tells the story of a "Good Samaritan." It is interesting to think about it as an example of how someone applied the Golden Rule to a situation he faced—and how some other people did not. Read Luke 10:25–37 with that in mind, and notice how the context also mentions the law, and uses the law in the ways we have discussed…

> And behold, a lawyer stood up to put him to the test, saying, "Teacher, what shall I do to inherit eternal life?" He said to him, "What is written in the Law? How do you read it?" And he answered, "You shall love the Lord your God with all your heart and with all your soul and with all your strength and with all your mind, and your neighbor as yourself." And he said to him, "You have answered correctly; do this, and you will live."
>
> But he, desiring to justify himself, said to Jesus, "And who is my neighbor?" Jesus replied, "A man was going down from Jerusalem to Jericho, and he fell among robbers, who stripped him and beat him and departed, leaving him half dead. Now by chance a priest was going down that road, and when he saw him he passed by on the other side. So likewise a Levite, when he came

to the place and saw him, passed by on the other side.

But a Samaritan, as he journeyed, came to where he was, and when he saw him, he had compassion. He went to him and bound up his wounds, pouring on oil and wine. Then he set him on his own animal and brought him to an inn and took care of him. And the next day he took out two denarii and gave them to the innkeeper, saying, 'Take care of him, and whatever more you spend, I will repay you when I come back.'

Which of these three, do you think, proved to be a neighbor to the man who fell among the robbers?" He said, "The one who showed him mercy." And Jesus said to him, "You go, and do likewise."

The lawyer who questioned Jesus clearly thought that he had kept the law—which, of course, no one can do. Jesus' story was intended to make that clear. Thinking about this from the perspective of the Golden Rule, we might say that Jesus told the story of a man who practiced the Golden Rule to show the lawyer his sin. The lawyer was "wishing to justify himself," and he hoped that when Jesus said, "love your neighbor," he meant "love the people who loved you"—or perhaps, "love the people you like or find attractive." The law-yer may have done that quite successfully—we don't know. But there was no way he or anyone else would be able to love his *enemies* consistently, if at all.

Yet "love your enemies" is exactly what God has told us to do (Matt. 5:44, Luke 6:35). So Jesus responded to the lawyer's question by telling him a story about a man who *did* love his enemy. Would it be someone religious—a priest, or a Levite—who helped his fellow countryman? We might have expected one of those two to show love in that way; but, in fact, the only one who did was the Samaritan—and, as everyone listening to Jesus' story would have known, they were hated and mistreated by the Jews.

Some people think the story of the Good Samaritan is an example of how good works can make us deserving of heaven. But it's really making the opposite point: even the most "spiritual" people don't keep the law like they should.

And so, each one of us needs a representative Savior who can do for us what we cannot do for ourselves—someone who can keep the law perfectly and experience death in our place, paying the penalty we owe for breaking the law.

Even though the main point of the parable is to show us our need for salvation through Christ, the story also tells us what we should do, as Christians, to please God. After describing the Samaritan's acts of kindness in detail, Jesus says "Go and do the same." Showing love to others, particularly needy people, is the essence of what it means to live as a believer in Christ, in gratefulness to him who has been so merciful to us (Jer. 22:13–16, Micah 6:8, Matt. 25:31–48, 1 John 3:17).

One of the definitions of *Christian* in Webster's dictionary is "having or showing the qualities that Christians are supposed to have, such as kindness, charity, and humbleness."[9] The book of James makes

> *Each one of us needs a representative Savior who can do for us what we cannot do for ourselves.*

a similar point when it says, "This is pure and undefiled religion in the sight of our God and Father, to visit orphans and widows in their distress" (1:27).

The social responsibility implied in that verse is also implied in Jesus' famous story. What do you think would happen in society at large if more people acted like the Good Samaritan, rather than the priest and Levite who were thinking only of themselves? There would be far fewer hurting people in the world, that's for sure.

This parable illustrates the purposes and benefits of the law, and of the Golden Rule, as well as any story ever told.

Rightly Understanding the Rule

To understand the Rule and apply it rightly to our lives, we need a deep and complete understanding of it, in the context of the rest of Scripture. And we want to avoid falling into some of the problems that have plagued many well-meaning people who have tried to live by it.

Versions of the Golden Rule appear in other religions and traditions, as we'll discuss further in Chapter Three, but those people are certainly not following it in its true, biblical sense. Sociologist Jeffrey Wattles gives some examples:

> Some Hindus interpret the injunction to treat others as oneself as an invitation to identify with the divine spirit within each person. Some Muslims take the Golden Rule to apply primarily [or only] to the brotherhood of Islam… And countless people think of the rule without any religious associations at all.[10]

Even among those who claim to be Christians, the wording of the Rule itself has sometimes been misunderstood—especially when it's considered in isolation from the larger context of Scripture. Liberal theologian Paul Tillich, for example, "found the rule an inferior principle. For him, the biblical commandment to love and the assurance that God is love 'infinitely transcend' the Golden Rule. The problem with the rule is that it does not tell us what we *should* wish."[11] But the rest of Scripture does, of course—so Tillich's lack of faith in the full inspiration of Scripture kept him from commending this particular part.

Along the same lines, Wattles mentions a question that his students often ask: "What if a sadomasochist goes forth to treat others as he wants to be treated?" He adds, "It has been objected that the Golden Rule assumes that humans are basically alike and thereby

> We need to interpret and apply the Golden Rule very carefully, relating it to its larger context and especially to the truth of the gospel.

fails to do justice to the differences between people. In particular, the Rule allegedly implies that what we want is what others want. As George Bernard Shaw quipped, "Don't do to others as you want them to do to you. Their tastes may be different."[12]

There are good answers to objections like these, and we will discuss them in Chapter Three. Most of them have to do with the fact that the rest of Scripture provides a consistent standard for the application of the Rule. But, for now, the reason I mention them is to illustrate the fact that we need to interpret and apply the Golden Rule very carefully, relating it to its larger context and especially to the truth of the gospel. As you will see in the next chapter, although the Social Gospel movement was ostensibly based on the Golden Rule, I believe it failed to interpret it and apply it carefully.

What Would You Do?

Carefully applied, the Golden Rule is a key to all kinds of situations. Here are some examples of real-life scenarios, all of which will be addressed late in this book:

- Your friend seems to have a drinking problem. He can't get to sleep at night without having a few. You can't remember any time he's only had one. You're pretty sure he's been over the legal limit several times when driving. But you're also pretty sure he will be very upset with you if you even imply that there is something wrong in this part of his life—and of course you've got your own vices. Who are you to say anything about him? What should you do? (Chapter Three)

- A young lady is dating a young man, who wants to "make out" with her in the car but promises to stop short of anything "really bad." He obviously has a strong desire to add this facet to their relationship, and she gets the impression that if she says no he will not want to continue dating her, because he doesn't just want another friend—he wants a girlfriend. She really likes him and she doesn't want to lose him. What should she do? (Chapter Three)

- You've noticed some bad behavior by a child in the church, which seems to have gone unaddressed by his parents on numerous occasions. You've thought about talking to the parents about this, but you don't know them very well and you're afraid that would cause an uncomfortable rift between you and them. What should you do? (Chapter Four)

- You helped a man with his bills one month, and now he is asking for help the next month, but you're not sure how he spends his money and he's unwilling to meet with someone for financial counsel. Should you help him a second time? (Chapter Five)

- A woman approaches you in the city subway system, asking you to buy her a ticket so she can take the train home. Nothing about her seems suspicious. What should you do? (Chapter Five)

The Real Secret

Understanding and applying the Golden Rule rightly will help us in all those scenarios, in one way or another. In fact, a *right* understanding and application of it could settle the issue in most of them. At the very least, thinking about the Golden Rule in those situations will direct our minds away from our own desires and focus it on the needs of others, setting us on the right path toward true godliness. It will also make us realize how much we need God's help to be truly godly! The Golden Rule is truly a priceless key that unlocks eternal treasure in our relationships with other people, and with God.

The great escape artist Houdini generated interest in his traveling show by arriving early in a town and offering the local jailers $1,000 if he could not get out of their jail in less than an hour. In one town, Houdini was ushered into a cell, and after the door clanged shut and the officers left, he immediately began trying to find a way out. He soon realized that this jail was going to be tougher than usual, and after trying every trick he knew, he gave up and sat down in the middle of the

> *The Golden Rule is truly a priceless key that unlocks eternal treasure in our relationships with other people, and with God.*

cell, sobbing in frustration. He had failed miserably. When the officers returned an hour later to let him out, they realized that, in their excitement at having the famous man there, they had forgotten to lock the door of the cell! Houdini had tried and tried to escape without success, but all he needed to do was open the cell door and walk right out.[13]

That is how many of us are when it comes to the problems and challenges we face in life. We try all kinds of things to improve our relationships with other people and with God, while forgetting this very important key—the Golden Rule. Rediscovering it and putting it into practice will prove it to be truly golden—not only because it's so valuable but because it gives us a reliable standard on which to base our life's choices.

Questions for Thought and Discussion

1. The Golden Rule summarizes the law of God. Why is the law of God so important in our lives?

2. We are not saved by keeping the law, but it plays a necessary role in our salvation. Why can we not be saved without the law?

3. Many people mistakenly view the story of the Good Samaritan as teaching us how to be a good person who deserves to go to heaven. How is the main purpose of the story really the opposite of that?

4. The Golden Rule can help us in addressing problems we face in life. What is an example of a difficult challenge you face right now in your relationship with another person? How might the Golden Rule help you?

two

TARNISHED

How the Golden Rule Was Lost for Generations

Sam "Golden Rule" Jones, whom we met briefly in the previous chapter, was a well-known businessman, politician, and social reformer in the early twentieth century in America. The oil companies and factory he owned at one time in his career had only one rule—the Golden Rule—which he endeavored to practice in all aspects of his relations with his workers. He pioneered the eight-hour day for well drillers, saying that following the Golden Rule with his workers was more important than his company making money.

> In the company cafeteria a worker could get a hot lunch for fifteen cents (the "Golden Rule Dinner") which cost the company twenty-one cents to prepare. The rationale for the dinner, Jones explained, was fellowship, good nourishment, and sparing the worker's wife the effort and cost of making an extra lunch... Jones needed a foundry,

but when he acquired the property adjacent to his factory he turned the land into Golden Rule Park instead. The park was made available to his workers and their families. They met there evenings and Sunday afternoons to picnic, listen to speeches, and enjoy concerts performed by the Golden Rule Band. A large room in the factory was converted into a meeting room, Golden Rule Hall.[14]

The fact that Jones and others like him referred to the Golden Rule so often is an evidence of its widespread popularity. In addition, Jones and the rest of the Golden Rule fraternity were very influential in spreading the use of the Rule and adding to its reputation. It was truly an element of the foundation of American society at the time, and widely seen as a significant key to relationships.

Today, however, it's a different story. An extensive web search of books in print reveals only two available works on the Golden Rule (one by Wattles and one by Harry Gensler).[15] The authors are not pastors or teachers of religion, they're philosophy professors. This is amazing when you consider the tidal wave of books that flood from our publishing houses every day, with multiple titles about every topic imaginable. For instance, a search I did for *cheese* on the Barnes and Noble website yielded 1,307 items, and I saw an entire hundred-page book on the topic of Athlete's Foot! On Christianbook.com, the topic "speaking in tongues" yielded 116 results, and *money* can be found in the title of 704 Christian books. In fact, if you enter *money* as a keyword, you are presented with more than 2,300 resources on the subject! Clearly there is much more interest today in the "rule of gold" than in the Golden Rule.

This maxim that Jesus mentions twice in the Gospels, a maxim that Jesus calls a summary of the whole Old Testament, and one that was familiar to almost everybody in our culture a hundred years ago, has now faded into obscurity and obsolescence—among

We can learn so much from looking at the mistakes Christians have made—and the over-reactions of others to those mistakes.

evangelicals, in particular. My investigation into why this happened has produced interesting insights, and I believe that an understanding of the decline of the Golden Rule contains the seeds of its recovery. Knowing the history behind its departure from the minds and hearts of Christians can help bring about its return. We can learn so much from looking at past events, especially at the mistakes that Christians have made— and the over-reactions of others to those mistakes. Or to put it negatively, he who does not know history is doomed to repeat it.

So, this chapter will discuss six reasons why the Golden Rule has passed out of use among evangelical Christians—or, to put it another way, six causes for its disappearance from our collective consciousness. And while we do that, I will also suggest some responses to those reasons, and some cures for the causes. And in doing so we will hopefully begin to understand the real meaning and application of this lost key to relationships.

The first three reasons addressed below—each one an *ism*—are primarily ideological (liberalism, socialism, and various types of millennialism). The second three, as we'll see, are more practical and personal.

Reason One
The Golden Rule Became Associated with Liberalism

By *liberalism*, I mean theological rather than political liberalism. Theological liberalism (also called "progressivism") is basically the view that the Bible is not entirely true in everything it says. To liberals, the Bible is more human than divine, and they do not believe that in Scripture God inspired a *perfect* revelation of his will and ways. So, as a result, they believe that many ideas in the Bible need to be "updated" in the light of modern science, psychology, and morality. Conservative evangelicals, on the other hand, accept the Bible as equally human and divine—just as Jesus Christ, the living Word, is both human and divine—and trust it to be the truth of God in everything it says.

Unfortunately for the Golden Rule, most of its most vocal proponents in the social reform movement of the early 1900s were theological liberals. The Golden-Rule-quoting liberals were seen as a threat to evangelical faith and, as a result, most conservative Christians dismissed the movement and its main slogan. *The liberals are always talking about the Golden Rule*, they thought, consciously or sub-consciously. *We don't want to be liberal, so we shouldn't talk about the Golden Rule.*[16]

Walter Rauschenbusch, a Baptist minister and author, was widely known as the primary religious thinker of the movement. In 1917 he wrote its most well-known doctrinal defense, *A Theology for the Social Gospel.* Although he claimed to be standing in the line of orthodoxy, this book did not define sin, salvation, and even lesser issues like baptism, in the same way as historic Protestantism did, or even Catholicism for that matter. George Herron, another prominent spokesman for the movement (and the Golden Rule) started out as a Congregationalist pastor but ended up leaving the ministry to join the Socialist Party and divorced his wife in the midst of an adultery scandal. He later repudiated marriage itself as an aberrant invention of man. Even Sam "Golden Rule" Jones, who seemed to have an exemplary personal character, rejected the idea of church and never attended one. He also sadly misunderstood the biblical gospel, saying cringeworthy things like this: "Neither Moses nor Jesus nor Lincoln nor any other man or woman ever saved the people. All they could do or did was live the ideal life that each one must live in order to save himself."[17]

These were the kinds of men who represented the social reform movement of the early 1900s and quoted the Golden Rule at every opportunity. As a result, the Rule itself became associated with their brand of mod-

The liberals were right that the Golden Rule calls us to meet the needs of those less fortunate than ourselves. But they often neglected the priority of holy living, and failed to define faith in a biblically orthodox way.

ernism, and it began to leave a bad taste in the mouths of conservative Christians, who rightly opposed liberal perversions of "the faith that was once for all delivered to the saints" (Jude 3).

But this "guilt by association"—whose unfortunate effects continue to this day—is not necessary or justified. It wasn't just liberals who advocated the Golden Rule. There have been many conservative,

Bible-believing Christians who have also taught and practiced the Golden Rule, even during the social reform movement of the early 1900s. They did so because the Bible teaches the Golden Rule. Not only that, but the Bible also emphasizes the kind of social work that was advocated by the liberals and others. The Bible even says that it is part of the essence of the Christian faith—or at least a necessary evidence of personal faith. Consider these verses from the book of James:

> Religion that is pure and undefiled before God the Father is this: to visit orphans and widows in their affliction, and to keep oneself unstained from the world. (1:27).

> What good is it, my brothers, if someone says he has faith but does not have works? Can that faith save him? If a brother or sister is poorly clothed and lacking in daily food, and one of you says to them, "Go in peace, be warmed and filled," without giving them the things needed for the body, what good is that? So also faith by itself, if it does not have works, is dead. (2:14–17, see also 1 John 3:17)

The liberals were right that the Golden Rule calls us to meet the needs of those less fortunate than ourselves. However, they often neglected the priority of holy living and failed to define faith in a biblically orthodox way. What's more, because of their neglect, something even worse happened: genuine Christians threw the baby out with the bathwater. This was understandable—because the bathwater was not only dirty with liberalism, but also with another scary *ism*…

Reason Two

The Golden Rule Became Associated with Socialism

Webster's dictionary defines *socialism* as "any of various theories or systems in which the means of producing and distributing goods are owned and operated by society rather than private individuals."[18] A religious version of this political philosophy, known as Christian Socialism, was advocated by many of the people who quoted and promoted the Golden Rule in the early part of the twentieth century. At that time in America, socialism appealed to many Christians as an answer to the greed and injustice that had run rampant during the Industrial Age. Leo Tolstoy, a Russian intellectual who wrote the famous novels *War and Peace* and *Anna Karenina*, became very influential among thinkers in the West when he denounced all worldly pleasures (including private property) and basically lived the life of an ascetic monk among the rural peasants in his homeland. Many Western Christians considered his anarchist critiques of war and capitalism to be prophetic, and much hope for social change among the Golden Rule reformers was founded on the ideas of Tolstoy and some other seminal thinkers, like the Italian collectivist Giuseppe Mazzini. Walter Rauschenbusch, for example, "believed that if the rich man would not give up his riches voluntarily by an act of personal renunciation, such as Jesus and Tolstoy enjoined, then a reorganized society would be compelled (and would have the right) to take his wealth away forcibly and share it with others."[19]

Notice in that quote the idea of *compulsory* redistribution of wealth, which became an integral part of socialist theory in the following decades and played a key role in the history of the twentieth century. The third definition of *socialism* in Webster's dictionary alludes to this, calling it "the stage of society, in Marxist doctrine, coming between the capitalist stage and the communist stage, in which private ownership of the means of production and distribution has been done away with."

The bathwater of socialism got really dirty when Karl Marx and Vladimir Lenin catalyzed the Communist Revolution in Russia and the birth of the atheistic Soviet Union. Then when China took the same route—moving from discussions of socialism to a violent, oppressive, anti-Christian Communist regime—believers in the West (among others) became horrified at the thought of both socialism and communism.

Princeton Seminary professor William Greene had seen the writing on the wall as far back as 1908. Historian Gary Scott Smith writes:

> Christians must repudiate socialism, William Greene declared, because it would give too much power to the state. Socialism substituted "state control for providence" and put "society in the place of God." Worse yet, he protested, increased state regulation and intervention threatened to lead to "worship of the state" and suppression of individual initiative. If the state owned the means of production, Greene asked, what was to prevent it from assuming supremacy in other spheres of life as well?[20]

Anyone who knows anything about later twentieth-century world history can plainly see that Greene was a prophet in this regard. The Communist regimes in Russia and China did in fact come to embody all his predictions, and when they did, people in the West had all the more reason to reject not only Communism, but the socialistic thinking that led to it.

The Golden Rule, since it was so often quoted by socialists, suffered from "guilt by association" and was thrown out with the bathwater. The logic is understandable: The Golden Rule was important to those who wanted to change our way of life to something that is dangerous and ineffective, so maybe the Golden Rule itself is somehow dangerous and ineffective.

But the Golden Rule can be applied to business and politics without necessarily leading to socialism. The Golden Rule does imply that the wealthy should have less and the needy more. However, that is because the wealthy should *voluntarily* share their wealth—not because the government or anyone else forces them to do so.

This distinction is an important one. In the Star Trek movie *The Wrath of Khan*, Mr. Spock sacrifices himself to save the whole crew of the *Enterprise* because "the needs of the many outweigh the needs of the few." That is a biblical principle, and his action was a righteous one. But imagine if Spock had not wanted to make that sacrifice—and Captain Kirk ordered him to do it! There would be something wrong with that. The problem with most forms of socialism is not the redistribution of wealth *per se*, but the forcible redistribution of wealth.

The Bible teaches these principles in various places—as an example, consider the eight and tenth commandments in Exodus 20. There, God says, "You shall not steal" (v. 15) and "You shall not covet your neighbor's house; you shall not covet your neighbor's wife or his male servant or his female servant or his ox or his donkey or anything that belongs to your neighbor" (v. 17). The right to own private property is confirmed by those verses, and the implication throughout the rest of Scripture is that only God himself could ever rightfully take it away. For example, in 1 Samuel 8:10–18, the idea of a king (or any kind of government) taking things from people is a bad idea, according to God. Six times in that passage God says, "he will take," with the result being that the people will "cry out" in anguish and regret (v. 18).

On the other hand, look at how the voluntary, sacrificial giving of God's people was pleasing to him in these passages describing the early church:

> And all who believed were together and had all things in common. And they were selling their possessions and belongings and distributing the proceeds to all, as any had need. (Acts 2:44–45)

> Now the full number of those who believed were of one heart and soul, and no one said that any of the things that belonged to him was his own, but they had everything in common.... There was not a needy person among them, for as many as were owners of lands or houses sold them and brought the proceeds of what was sold and laid it at the apostles' feet, and it was distributed to each as any had need. (Acts 4:32–35)

On the surface these passages might be thought to support socialistic or even communistic ideology. But a closer look at them, bearing in mind the broader context of Scripture, reveals that this sacrificial "redistribution of wealth" was entirely voluntary on the part of the early Christians. The text never says that the ownership of private property was wrong, nor does it say they were required to sell it. Having "all things in common" is best understood as an *attitude* of caring and sharing, because we know from elsewhere in the New Testament that Christians continued to own properties and businesses—for example, Priscilla and Aquila in Romans 16:3–5 and Lydia in Acts 16:14–15. In fact, in 1 Timothy 6:17–18, Paul instructs the rich

*The problem with most forms of socialism is not the redistribution of wealth **per se**, but the forcible redistribution of wealth.*

people in Ephesus to share, but he never tells them it is wrong to be rich, or that they should give everything away. Even Ananias and Sapphira, in the story directly following the Acts 4 passage, were not punished by God for keeping the money for themselves, but because they "lied to the Holy Spirit" (Acts 5:3–4).

Also, the radical sacrificial giving by the early church described in Acts was not necessarily the norm for all times and places, but was in response to an extreme need that had arisen. Many of the Jews at Pentecost who had believed in Christ at Pentecost were now cut off from their families and livelihoods and stuck in Jerusalem with no means of caring for themselves. This is why Paul spent so much time gathering offerings for the "poor in Jerusalem" on his missionary journeys (see 2 Cor. 8–9).

The *principles* of giving generously and sacrificially, caring for the poor, and even viewing what we have as "not our own" apply directly to Christians in all ages and situations. But the specific circumstances in the early chapters of Acts cannot be made to support the idea of governmental seizure of private property, which is what *communism* means and what *socialism* often includes. And there is clearly no reason to associate the Golden Rule with those *isms*, as many Christians mistakenly and unfortunately have done.

That brings us to some other *isms*…

Reason Three
The Golden Rule Was Eclipsed by a Shift in End-Time Views

In the early 1900s, most professing Christians believed the world was getting better. Liberals and socialists generally had a high view of humanity's innate goodness and an optimism about our progress, which was fueled by Darwinism and seemingly confirmed by the advances of the Industrial Revolution. Most evangelical Christians—or, at least, most of the influential theologians of the day—shared this optimism, although their reasons for hope were very different.

The burgeoning worldwide missions movement

gave them cause for optimism—as did their belief in a postmillennial eschatology. Postmillennialism is a perspective about the future that says Jesus will return to earth after his people have ushered in a golden age of Christianity, where most of the world will be converted to Christ, and most of its institutions conformed to Christian principles. The progress that evangelicals were seeing in the world around them may not have been the *reason* why so many of them believed in postmillennialism—they would have said it is a biblical concept—but the progress around them certainly seemed to confirm it in their minds.

Then came "dispensational premillennialism," a new perspective on history popularized by men such as Dwight L. Moody, Lewis Sperry Chafer of Dallas Seminary, and C. I. Scofield of the *Scofield Reference Bible*. These teachers and their adherents believed that the Bible predicts the decline and deterioration of social, political, and economic conditions in the world, ending in the Rapture of the Church, the Great Tribulation, and the Second Coming of Christ, who will *then* establish his kingdom on the earth (hence "*pre*millennial"). This would be the culmination of different dispensations of time throughout history (hence "dispensational").

Premillennialism had existed before, often in more culturally optimistic versions, but this dispensational brand was typically pessimistic about the progress of society, believing that only the return of Christ could make the world a better place. So Moody, for instance, was known for his "declaration that Christians must focus exclusively on saving souls because the world was a 'wrecked vessel.'"[21] In other words, evangelism was what mattered the most, because social action would ultimately be pointless. Other leading premillennialists joined him in asserting that "social reforms

*The progress that evangelicals were seeing in the world around them may not have been the **reason** why so many of them believed in postmillennialism— they would have said it is a biblical concept—but the progress around them certainly seemed to confirm it in their minds.*

were worthless, futile, and foolish because, as I. M. Haldeman put it, *'the church is here to testify the world cannot be made better: that so far from being made better it will go from bad to worse.'"*[22]

Those who accepted this view had little confidence the Golden Rule could be successfully applied in these "last days." In fact, many of them believed that the whole Sermon on the Mount in Matthew 5–7 was intended only for the nation of Israel in its "dispensation of law," and was therefore not directly applicable to us in the "church age."[23] Dismissing the liberal Social Gospelers and disagreeing with the cultural optimism of postmillennial evangelicals, dispensational premillennialists were not too keen on the Golden Rule, seeing it as a slogan associated with unbiblical theologies. As a result, they did not refer to it much—and when they did, it was often in the context of criticizing those who misused or overemphasized it.[24]

Dispensational premillennialists were in the minority in the early 1900s, so their aversion to the Golden Rule did not affect its widespread understanding and use at that time. But two factors propelled the popularity of this belief system among evangelical Christians in America, so that by the middle of the century it had become the majority view, at least among most conservative evangelicals.

First, dispensationalists emphasized a literal interpretation of the Old Testament prophecies and promises to Israel. This appealed to the masses of sincere believers, who were either scared or tired of liberals saying that much of the Bible was not literally true (for example, the miracles recorded in it). Viewing the Old Testament promises as "figurative" or "typological"—as other conservative Christians did—sounded too much like liberalism to many Christians. As a result, they flocked to dispensationalism for what they thought was a consistently conservative approach to interpreting the Bible.[25]

The second major factor in the rise of dispensational premillennialism was the devastation of the two World Wars. World War I seriously wounded the idea that the human race was getting better, and World War II basically killed it. The horrors of those two wars visited every home by way of the growing news media. Fewer and fewer Christians could imagine the kingdom of Christ developing through the work of humans on the earth. More and more could only conceive of it happening by a cataclysmic return of the King himself. World events seemed to confirm dispensational views of the end times—particularly the re-establishment of a Jewish nation in 1948, which dispensational leaders had predicted would happen before Christ returned. Thus, a powerful sense of prophetic fulfillment came to be associated with dispensationalism, causing it to eclipse more traditional theological perspectives, especially those that had a more optimistic view of the future.

So, postmillennialism declined among Christians in the mid-1900s—and, with it, the Golden Rule, which had been quoted so much by those who thought the world would become a better place. They had apparently been proven wrong by world events, and it seemed that their favorite slogan was permanently tainted.

However, the idea that the world will *necessarily* grow worse and worse until Christ returns is debatable.[26] And even if it is true, that still doesn't mean we shouldn't emphasize and practice the Golden Rule in the meantime, even for the purpose of improving society. The same portions of the Bible that contain the best-known prophecies of decline also contain injunctions to social service and mercy ministry based on the Golden Rule. For example, right after Jesus' predictions of tribulation in Matthew 24 comes his sheep-and-goats parable in Matthew 25:31–48, where he says that true believers are characterized by caring

> *The same portions of the Bible that contain the best-known prophecies of decline also contain injunctions to social service and mercy ministry based on the Golden Rule.*

for the needy. In his pastoral epistles, Paul says that "evil men and impostors will proceed from bad to worse" (2 Tim. 3:13), but also says that wealthy people are "to do good, to be rich in good works, to be generous and ready to share" (1 Tim. 6:18). And as the next reason reveals, the Golden Rule is not just about "improving society" or meeting the physical needs of people, it has a much deeper, spiritual purpose that should be exciting to anyone who loves the gospel of Jesus Christ.

Reason Four

Proponents of the Golden Rule Often Emphasized the Physical at the Expense of the Spiritual

Or we could say they emphasized the earthly at the expense of the heavenly, as illustrated by the life of the famous social progressive George Herron. He left his ministry as a pastor and theological professor to join the socialist party and devote his life to politics. His passion for the Golden Rule seemed to lead him away from Christ and the church, and that was a trend many Christians were rightly concerned about.[27]

Bible-believing critics of the Social Gospel movement pointed out that the Bible says, "You must be born again" (John 3:7), not "You must be reformed again." They felt it necessary to remind their listeners again and again that the Golden Rule is *not* the gospel, because those who quoted it a lot were often confusing the two. They wanted to make sure people knew that only "the simple Gospel, the story of the cross" had "the power to save man and better conditions."[28] Their message was that "the mission of the church was not to purify Sodom but to proclaim the Savior.... These convictions led conservatives to assert repeatedly and vehemently that the most effective way to improve society was to evangelize the unsaved."[29]

These criticisms of the social progress movement

were well-founded and important. The Golden Rule is not the gospel, and no real good will ever come of it if we focus only on people's outward actions, without addressing the heart. So, as we rediscover the Golden Rule and emphasize it again, we need to remember that our primary goal should be spiritual change.

And spiritual change is precisely what the Golden Rule is intended to accomplish when it is understood and used rightly. Remember that the Golden Rule is a summary of the law of God—and the primary purpose for the law of God is to show us our sin, so that we will run to the Savior.

For example, consider the story in 2 Samuel 12:1-7 of when the prophet Nathan confronted King David for his sins of adultery and murder. Nathan told David a story of a rich man with many sheep who stole the one little lamb belonging to a poor man; Nathan then went on to explain how David had done the same thing to Uriah by stealing his wife from him. In doing so, the prophet was basically applying the Golden Rule, long before Jesus even spoke it. He was showing David why his actions were wrong by causing him to think more objectively about the matter, making him see things through the eyes of another. He was saying to David, in a creative way, "Would you want to be treated in this way?" And it worked. David realized how wrong he had been and finally confessed his sin (2 Sam. 12:13, Psa. 32:5). Though he and the nation did suffer the consequences of his sin (2 Sam. 12:14), he was able to retain his throne and the nation was not utterly destroyed by God.

Nathan's creative use of the Golden Rule enabled him to show David the seriousness of his sin and his need for forgiveness. It even led David to the free justification that comes through the substitutionary sacrifice of Christ. Notice how David learned these things as a result of his "Golden Rule" confrontation:

> Blessed is the one whose transgression is forgiven, whose sin is covered. Blessed is the man against whom the Lord counts no iniquity, and in whose spirit there is no deceit. (Psa. 32:1–2)

> For you will not delight in sacrifice, or I would give it; you will not be pleased with a burnt offering. The sacrifices of God are a broken spirit; a broken and contrite heart, O God, you will not despise.
>
> Do good to Zion in your good pleasure; build up the walls of Jerusalem; then will you delight in right sacrifices, in burnt offerings and whole burnt offerings; then bulls will be offered on your altar. (Psa. 51:16–19)

The Psalm 32 passage is quoted in the middle of Paul's great treatise in Romans on justification by faith (Rom. 4:7–8) as an example of what it means to trust in Christ rather than our own works. And the Psalm 51 verses are part of David's famous prayer of repentance in Psalm 51, which he prayed after Nathan confronted him and then wrote down for our instruction. In those verses, I believe David is looking forward to and foreshadowing the cross of Christ—when he talks about the "righteous sacrifices" that alone can atone for sin. In the kind of prophetic typology that is often found in the Old Testament, he is speaking of the coming messianic age, when sacrifices would be truly acceptable to God for the first time because they were offered by his Son. But regardless of whether or not such typology is present in this psalm, it is clear that the effect of applying the Golden Rule to David's life was to make him realize his sin and need for salvation. And as a result, he became a kinder and more caring king.

A reading of David's life story from 1 Samuel 16 to 1 Kings 2 shows that he was a different man after being confronted by Nathan. Before that, he repeatedly slaughtered all his enemies, down to the very last man (for example, 1 Sam. 27:9), and in one of the few cases where he did not, he made his enemies lie down and randomly killed two out of every three, enslaving the rest (2 Sam. 8:2). He was also about to kill Nabal and every male in his clan merely because the man insulted him, until Nabal's wife Abigail interceded for her family (1 Sam. 25). After David realized the depth of his sin with Bathsheba, however, he showed mercy to some of his critics and enemies (2 Sam. 16:11, 19:22–23, 29, 38). He wept bitterly in mourning for his sons Amnon and Absalom (2 Ki. 13), even though one had raped his sister and the other had rebelled against David and tried to kill him. And at the end of his life, David wanted to suffer instead of the people (2 Sam.

> *Nathan's creative use of the Golden Rule enabled him to show David the seriousness of his sin and his need for forgiveness.*

24:17)—another picture of Christ—and he insisted on paying an honorable man for goods that were offered to him for free (2 Sam. 24:24).

It was Nathan's creative application of God's law to David's sin that caused David to see his need for grace, and subsequently made him a more gracious man. That is why the Golden Rule is the lost key to relationships—because of what it can do when it is accompanied by the power of the Holy Spirit. It does not merely change or inform our outward behavior. It first convicts our hearts about how we have not loved others as ourselves. Then, as we look to Christ for the forgiveness and grace we need, we are transformed by the Spirit and motivated by gratefulness to love others more. We will want to meet their needs in Christ's name and will not be content with merely "playing church" or keeping blessings to ourselves. We will want to make a difference in our society, not because social action *is* the gospel, but *because* of the gospel.

Finally, while Golden Rule living should never replace evangelism, it can powerfully aid that essential ministry of the church. Jesus said, "By this all people will know that you are My disciples, if you have love for one another" (John 13:35), and the early church's compassionate care for its widows was part of the reason for the mass conversions they experienced, which included "a great many of the priests" (Acts 6:1–7). This probably happened because the priests were the ones in Israel who had been given the responsibility of caring for the needy, and they were amazed that someone else was actually doing it! The physical ministries that flow from a commitment to the Golden Rule and the spiritual ministry of evangelism are not mutually exclusive—and, therefore, not a reason to reject the Golden Rule. When practiced biblically, these physical and spiritual ministries complement one another.

Reason Five

Proponents of the Rule Often Applied It Poorly to Business and Society

A fifth reason why many evangelicals turned their backs on the Golden Rule stems from the failure of its proponents to practice it successfully. Although we can still see some fruit from the efforts of the social reformers, the ones who touted the Golden Rule were more acquainted with failure than success during their own time. One of the themes of Peter Fredericks' book, *Knights of the Golden Rule,* is that all the ten reformers he describes were tragic figures, because they all ended up discouraged and disillusioned in their attempts to apply the Rule to various institutions in society. Although many people talked about the Golden Rule incessantly, very few actually practiced it. As Smith explains:

> In the 1920s the Golden Rule was widely heralded as the basic principle of business. Many codes of business ethics referred to it; shops, stores, and factories like J. C. Penney, the Golden Rule Department Store of St. Paul, ACIPCO, and the A. Nash Company professed to operate by it; and numerous books and articles discussed the maxim's relevance to commerce and industry. While many businessmen praised the Golden Rule as an ideal, Lunden argues, "few tried to live by it".... Most businessmen concluded, however, that this principle either could not be appropriately applied to business practices or else that it must be significantly modified in commercial settings. A survey in 1926, for example, asked 2,000 businessmen: "Can a man be successful in business today and practice the Golden Rule?" Only three percent of those who responded said yes.[30]

After all the sloganeering and blustering, the Golden

Rule just didn't seem to work. It was weighed in the balances of experience and found wanting. The movers and shakers of society had "tried" the Rule and, in their minds, it had failed. Like Prohibition, the other "noble experiment" of its time, the Golden Rule was eventually abandoned as a solution to the problems of the day. But the failure was more a result of man's sin

> *After all the sloganeering and blustering, the Golden Rule just didn't seem to work. It was weighed in the balances of experience and found wanting.*

than a failure God's truth. People thought the principle didn't work, but it was really the people who were broken.

For example, Walter Rauschenbusch and George Herron, the two most prominent liberal theologians who championed the Golden Rule, both ended up miserably disappointed. Rauschenbusch wrote shortly before he died, "since 1914 the world is full of hate, and I cannot expect to be happy again in my lifetime."[31] Six months before his death, Herron wrote that he had believed America "would establish a new world in which war would be forever ended and in which there would be a new human order that would be at least an approach to the kingdom of heaven.... Instead of the kingdom of heaven we have something nearer the kingdom of hell."[32]

What makes all this so interesting and applicable to us is that it illustrates an important truth about all the commandments of God: they have no power in themselves to change the hearts and lives of men. The Golden Rule "is the law," as Jesus said, and the law itself has never made anyone righteous or good. Consider these passages from the book of Romans:

> Now we know that whatever the law says it speaks to those who are under the law, so that every mouth may be stopped, and the whole world may be held accountable to God. For by works of the law no human being will be justified in his sight, since through the law comes knowledge of sin. (3:19–20)

> For while we were living in the flesh, our sinful passions, aroused by the law, were at work in our members to bear fruit for death. But now we are released from the law, having died to that which held us captive, so that we serve in the new way of the Spirit and not in the old way of the written code. What then shall we say? That the law is sin? By no means! Yet if it had not been for the law, I would not have known sin. For I would not have known what it is to covet if the law had not said, "You shall not covet." But sin, seizing an opportunity through the commandment, produced in me all kinds of covetousness. For apart from the law, sin lies dead. (7:5–8)

> The mind that is set on the flesh is hostile to God, for it does not submit to God's law; indeed, it cannot. (8:7)

As those passages make clear, the law does not make anyone better. In fact, in a way, it makes us worse, because our sinful flesh wants to do what we are told not to do. So, when Golden Rule advocates who were not true Christians tried to practice it without the power of the indwelling Spirit, they failed miserably. And

The Golden Rule will only "work" when it is practiced by a heart that has been born again by the Spirit of God and trusts in Jesus Christ as he is presented to us in the gospel

anyone who expects others to do it, or tries to force them to, inevitably ends up frustrated. You cannot *make* people follow the Golden Rule, nor can you do it by yourself, without the power of the Spirit.

It is not surprising that the Golden Rule did not "work" as a solution to the problems of an unregenerate society because, without true conversion, it cannot be truly practiced. As J. Gresham Machen wrote:

> The persons to whom the Golden Rule is addressed are persons in whom a great change has been wrought—a change which fits them for entrance into the Kingdom of God. Such persons

will have pure desires; they, and they only, can safely do unto others as they would have others do unto them, for the things that they would have others do unto them are high and pure.[33]

Unlike the unregenerate, we who believe in Christ can be forgiven for our failures and empowered to live according to God's laws, including the Golden Rule. As Romans 8:1–4 says:

There is therefore now no condemnation for those who are in Christ Jesus. For the law of the Spirit of life has set you free in Christ Jesus from the law of sin and death. For God has done what the law, weakened by the flesh, could not do. By sending his own Son in the likeness of sinful flesh and for sin, he condemned sin in the flesh, in order that the righteous requirement of the law might be fulfilled in us, who walk not according to the flesh but according to the Spirit.

The Golden Rule will only "work" when it is practiced by a heart that has been born again by the Spirit of God and trusts in Jesus Christ as he is presented to us in the gospel (Rom. 1:16; 10:17).

Reason Six
The Golden Rule Is Contrary to Our Sinful Nature

The previous five reasons for the disappearance of the Golden Rule are related to particular events in the history of the twentieth century, but this last one can happen at any time, and does. In fact, it is the reason that this book may not succeed in restoring the use of the Golden Rule, even among those who take the time to read it. Fallen humans are selfish and greedy and don't want to hear about the Golden Rule, let alone live by it. As I suggested earlier, all of us by nature are much more inclined toward the materialistic "rule of gold" than to the Golden Rule—I know that about myself, and I see it in others. So this crucial key to relationships is available to us, but we may simply choose not to use it. We are glad to have people treat us as we want to be treated—but we are not so keen on treating others the way we would want to be treated. In fact, even when we do follow the Golden Rule, it is often for the wrong reasons.

When I was teaching my church about this topic, a man who worked at a local car dealership came to visit one Sunday. After hearing about how great the Golden Rule is, he asked if I would come to his workplace and conduct a seminar on how to follow it in the car business. I wondered about his motives when he said,

"We'll try it and see if it works." I had even more cause to wonder about his motives when I found out that another salesman had given him an article about a man who held the record for most car sales in a month, citing Jesus' maxim as one of his methods! My salesman friend was thinking that he could get rich using the Golden Rule. I had to explain to him that we shouldn't be doing it to achieve goals like that. Our primary goals should be the glory of God (1 Cor. 10:31) and the good of others (Rom. 15:2).

Practicing the Golden Rule is contrary to our sinful nature—and we fail to do it for the right reasons as well. That makes it *impossible for us to obey* in every situation. So it can be tempting to think, *What's the use?* and give up. But if we do that, we are missing the main point of the Golden Rule—and all the commandments of God. They are designed "to lead us to Christ, that we might be justified by faith" (Gal. 3:24). The reason we so desperately need to teach and

The great psalmist throws himself on the mercy of God in faith and then asks God to change his heart and actions by the power of the Holy Spirit

talk about the Golden Rule, and not be prevented by the fact that our sinful nature contradicts it or by any of the other reasons we have discussed, is this: God can and will use it to show us our need for the gospel, through which our hearts can then be transformed. The experience of a very famous Christian illustrates this:

> The writings of Martin Luther (1483-1546) show a striking and complex evolution in the interpretation of the Golden Rule. Perhaps Luther's first sermon as an Augustinian monk (1510 or 1512) was on the rule, and he drew from it an extreme and religiously terrifying moral demand. Emphasizing the importance of the positive formulation of the Golden Rule, he reasoned that we cannot conform to it merely by avoiding evil. It is necessary for our salvation that we do good, indeed, that we do all the good we can. He concluded that if we fall short, we are condemned to eternal punishment.
>
> As Luther came to a personal experience of salvation by grace through faith, he began to see the meaning of the Golden Rule through a new concept of love. Though in this life sin is never altogether extinguished — the believer is "always justified, always sinner" — faith enables one to receive, alongside the old human nature, as it were, the new humanity, akin to the original condition of Adam before the fall into sin. Love for God and the neighbor is a dominant theme of religious living, and even the sense of rule or law is transformed by spiritual experience. Scripture may

no longer be taken as a locus of laws prescribing meritorious works that the pious, conscientious mind can perform. Instead, Scripture is a medium of communication between God and humankind, full of commands and promises, especially the promise that faith—the gift of God—and faith alone is the means of our salvation. The sinner who is willing to trust in the promises of God emerges into joy and liberty.

For Luther, then, the faith-practice of the Golden Rule can hardly be comprehended as rule-following in a conventional sense. Good works are to spring from the believer as from a fountain of gratitude.[34]

So why has the Golden Rule been largely ignored by evangelicals in recent years? I have suggested the following reasons:

- it became associated with theological liberalism

- it became associated with socialism

- it was eclipsed by the rise of dispensational premillennialism

- its proponents emphasized the physical at the expense of the spiritual

- its proponents often failed to apply it effectively in business and society

- it is contrary to our sinful nature

Earlier in this chapter, we discussed the story of Nathan's "Golden Rule confrontation" of David, so it is fitting for it to end with some words from David's prayer of repentance that followed. Notice how the great psalmist throws himself on the mercy of God in faith and then asks God to change his heart and actions by the power of the Holy Spirit. This is what you and I must do if we are to understand and practice this key to relationships in the right way. I encourage you to pray along with David as you read Psalm 51:

> To the choirmaster. A Psalm of David, when Nathan the prophet went to him, after he had gone in to Bathsheba.
>
> Have mercy on me, O God, according to your steadfast love;
> according to your abundant mercy blot out my transgressions.
> Wash me thoroughly from my iniquity, and cleanse me from my sin!
>
> For I know my transgressions,
> and my sin is ever before me.
> Against you, you only, have I sinned
> and done what is evil in your sight,
> so that you may be justified in your words
> and blameless in your judgment.
> Behold, I was brought forth in iniquity,
> and in sin did my mother conceive me.

Behold, you delight in truth in the inward being,
and you teach me wisdom in the secret heart.

Purge me with hyssop, and I shall be clean;
wash me, and I shall be whiter than snow.
Let me hear joy and gladness;
let the bones that you have broken rejoice.
Hide your face from my sins,
and blot out all my iniquities.
Create in me a clean heart, O God,
and renew a right spirit within me.
Cast me not away from your presence,
and take not your Holy Spirit from me.
Restore to me the joy of your salvation,
and uphold me with a willing spirit.

Then I will teach transgressors your ways,
and sinners will return to you.

Questions for Thought and Discussion

1. The Golden Rule was tarnished in the minds of evangelical Christians because of its association with theological liberalism and socialism. This should not have caused believers to ignore or neglect this command of Christ. Why is that?

2. The prophet Nathan used the Golden Rule in 2 Samuel 12:1–7 to bring King David to repentance for

his sin. How did it change David's heart and actions, and even affect others around him?

3. *The Social Gospel movement of the early twentieth century ultimately failed because it was not based on true faith in Christ. What were some of the problems with it, and how can we avoid them today?*

4. *Practicing the Golden Rule for the right reasons is contrary to our sinful nature. What are some wrong motives we can have for doing it?*

5. *Martin Luther's first sermon may have been about the Golden Rule. How did his perspective on its meaning and application change through the years?*

three

BURNISHED

Recovering the Golden Rule for the Church Today

In the previous chapter, we considered how the Golden Rule was lost. This chapter and the next are about rediscovering and recovering it. What exactly is the meaning of Christ's key to relationships? How does he intend us to practice it? This chapter will focus primarily on understanding its meaning, which has been misunderstood by almost everyone.

Golden Rule is not a biblical term, and Jesus' maxim is never referred to that way in Scripture. Sometime during church history, the saying became known by that moniker. In 1958, textual scholar Bruce Metzger wrote that the first occurrence he could track down was a footnote in Edward Gibbon's classic *Decline and Fall of the Roman Empire* (late eighteenth century), where Gibbon castigates John Calvin for allowing the execution of the heretic Servetus, saying he "violated the Golden Rule of doing as he would be done by."[35] Metzger adds, "From the almost stereotyped manner of Gibbon's reference to it, one would suppose that he was alluding to some well-worn cliché. Perhaps some reader of these lines can trace its origin more precisely than the present writer has done."[36]

Sociologist Jeffrey Wattles did just that in researching his 1996 book, *The Golden Rule*. He found three seventeenth-century books by English Puritans that "gave the golden rule its name."[37] But regardless of who coined the term, they undoubtedly did so because of the prominent role the Rule plays in the ethical system of Christianity, and in that of other world religions.

The History of the Rule

Variant forms of the Golden Rule existed long before Jesus. Homer's *Odyssey* (eighth century BCE) contains a story where the nymph Calypso tells Ulysses that she will not harm him because she would not want that for herself. A few hundred years later, the ancient Chinese teacher Confucius (551–479 BCE) reportedly said, "Do not impose on others what you do not desire others to impose on you."[38] Many of his followers repeated the same idea throughout the centuries following. Plato exemplifies the teaching of Greek philosophers like Socrates and Aristotle when he writes in his *Laws*, "I would have no one touch my property... if I am a man of reason, I must treat the property of others in the same way."[39]

The ancient forms of the Golden Rule most

pertinent to our consideration of Christ's teaching are the ones from Judaism, just prior to Jesus' lifetime or coinciding with it. One well-known example is the Book of Tobit (second century BCE), which says, "What you hate, do not do to anyone."[40] A manuscript found among the Dead Sea Scrolls, from a little later, says that "whatever you do not want to be done to you, you shall not do to anyone else." And the most famous articulation of the Golden Rule at the time of Jesus is attributed to Rabbi Hillel: When asked for a summary of the Torah, he replied, "What is hateful to you, do not do to your neighbor; that is the whole Torah, while the rest is commentary thereon; go and learn it."

Perhaps you noticed as you read those antecedents of the Golden Rule that they all have one thing in common: they are *negatively* stated—they tell us what we should *not* do. (This is sometimes referred to as the Silver Rule). Almost all the examples of the Rule found in ancient writings prior to Christ have a negative formulation. When Jesus stated the principle *positively* in his teaching ("*do* unto others…"), this was clearly an intentional innovation on his part, and he undoubtedly had a purpose for it. The positive form of the command is much harder to live by consistently—in fact, it is impossible! Given our sinful nature, no one can *always* do what is best for others. And that leads us again to the primary purpose of the Golden Rule, and all the laws of God.

The Golden Rule and the Law

The reason for the difference between the negative formulations and Jesus' positive formulation is the role of the law in Christianity, compared to all other religions. In all other religions, the rules are there for us to keep so we may be good people and earn our way to heaven, paradise, or whatever other desirable destiny. This principle of "works righteousness," regardless of what it might be called, is basically the approach and perspective of everyone on the planet except the true Christian—yes, even agnostics and atheists, and

> *When Jesus stated the principle positively in his teaching ("do unto others..."), this was clearly an intentional innovation on his part, and he undoubtedly had a purpose for it.*

many errant forms of Christianity itself. They believe they will be saved (however they may choose to define salvation) because of *who they are* and *what they do.* But authentic Christian faith acknowledges that no one can become righteous by keeping the law—in fact, the law is given to show us our sin and our need of a Savior, who must do for us what we could never do for ourselves. We are not saved because of who we are or what we do; we are saved because of *who Christ is* and *what he has done* through his death and resurrection.

Notice how Jesus himself makes exactly this point in Luke 18:9–14:

> Now He also told this parable to certain ones who trusted in themselves that they were righteous, and viewed others with contempt: "Two men went up into the temple to pray, one a Pharisee, and the other a tax collector. The Pharisee stood and began praying in this regard to himself, 'God, I thank You that I am not like other people: swindlers, crooked, adulterers, or even like this tax collector. I fast twice a week; I pay tithes of all that I get.' But the tax collector, standing some distance away, was even unwilling to lift his eyes toward heaven, but was beating his breast, saying, 'God, be merciful to me, the sinner!' I tell you, this man went down to his house justified rather than the other; for everyone who exalts himself will be humbled, but he who humbles himself will be exalted."

What was the difference between those two men? The ultra-religious, moral Pharisee, whom Jesus said was not forgiven and not going to heaven, was trusting in who he was ("I am…") and what he did ("I fast and give") to make him acceptable to God. But the irreligious, immoral tax collector knew he had nothing to offer God, and recognized that he could only be made acceptable by an act of mercy on God's part. That man "went down to his house justified [forgiven for his sins and heading to heaven] rather than the other."

The Golden Rule and the Gospel

The fact that the Golden Rule is "law" (as opposed to "grace") is so important to a right understanding of the Rule because we must remember that, by itself, it can do nothing to change us or make us better people (see Chapter Two). For that to happen, the Golden Rule must be accompanied and informed by the gospel of Christ. The Rule is not designed to make us right with God—and we must not allow that to be even part of our motive in practicing it. And because a proper motive is a gratefulness to God for his free grace toward us, we must not practice it for purely selfish goals—like the car salesman I mentioned in the last chapter, who thought he might get rich by applying it to his work.

Remember that the Golden Rule is a summary of the law of God. Martin Luther explains the effect of the law, and therefore, the effect of the Rule as well:

> When a man is humbled by the law [or the rule], and brought to the knowledge of himself, then follows true repentance (for true repentance begins at the fear and judgment of God), and he sees himself to be so great a sinner that he can find no means how he may be delivered from his sin by his own strength, endeavor and works. Then he perceives well what Paul means when he says that man is the servant and bond-slave of sin

(Rom. 7:14); also that God has shut up all under sin (Rom. 11:32; Gal. 3:22) and that the whole world is guilty before God (Rom. 3:19).

Now the sinner begins to sigh, and say: who then can help me? Terrified by the law and utterly despairing of his own strength, he looks about and sighs for the help of another, of a mediator and savior. Then comes in good time the healthful word of the gospel, which says, "Son, thy sins be forgiven thee" (Matt. 9:2). Believe in Jesus Christ, crucified for your sins. If you feel your sins and their burden, look not upon them in yourself, but remember that they are translated and laid upon Christ, whose stripes have made you whole (Isaiah 53:5). This is the beginning of health and salvation. By this means we are delivered from sin, justified and made inheritors of eternal life, not for our own works and deserts, but for our faith, whereby we lay hold upon Christ.[41]

Realizing that we are sinners and looking to the Savior is not only "the beginning of health and salvation," as Luther said, but it is also the beginning of any true practice of the Golden Rule (and the rest of the law). When we look to Christ and trust in his gospel of grace, our hearts are transformed at the deepest level and we now *want* to obey the one who loves us so much! And we want to treat others the way we would want to be treated, because that is what he commands us to do.

What the Golden Rule Does Not Mean

As we continue to work toward an accurate and complete definition of the Golden Rule, we need to consider and correct some misunderstandings about it. The first and most important misunderstanding, of course, is the one we just discussed—that practicing it or any other good work is "the way to heaven." But there are other significant misunderstandings as well, and eliminating them will lead us toward a proper grasp of what Jesus was really teaching. Just as a treasure chest can't be unlocked with the wrong key, you won't enjoy truly good relationships if you have wrong ideas about the Golden Rule in your mind. So think through this carefully with me...

The Golden Rule is not about what the other person wants. This very common misunderstanding derives from a superficial reading of the command. And some have gone so far as to formulate what they call the Platinum Rule (at a minimum implying it is better than the Golden Rule), which is "treat others as *they* want to be treated." This is taught in business seminars and even in some churches, where the teachers think they can improve on the Master's teaching![42]

But Jesus does not say to "treat others as they want to be treated"—he says, "treat others as *you* would want to be treated." This is a significant difference, and it is also significantly better than the other formulation, because many times *the way other people want to be treated is not what is best for them.* Consider two of the examples I mentioned in Chapter One:

- Your friend can't get to sleep at night without having a few drinks. You can't remember any time he's only had one. You're pretty sure he's been over the legal limit several times when driving. But you're also pretty sure he will be very upset with you if you even imply that there is something wrong in this part of his life—and of course you've got your own vices. Who are you to say anything about him? What should you do?

- A young lady is dating a young man, who wants to "make out" with her in the car but promises to stop short of anything "really bad." He obviously has a strong desire to add this facet to their relationship, and she gets the impression that if she says no he will not want to continue dating her, because he doesn't just want another friend—he wants a girlfriend, as he understands that relationship. She really likes him and she doesn't want to lose him. What should she do?

If the Golden Rule was "treat others as they want to be treated," you would never confront the alcoholic friend, because he clearly doesn't want to be confronted. And the young lady would just give in to her date, because he definitely wants to dishonor her. But is it best for the alcoholic to go unconfronted, and is it best for the young couple to give in to temptation? The Scriptures would say no in both situations, because in both situations the people involved are headed for trouble and will surely be harmed if they stay on that path (see Prov. 23:29–35 and 1 Thess. 4:3–8).

When Jesus says to "treat others as you would want to be treated," he is bringing a greater measure of objectivity to the issue. A person's desires are subjective and often biased by their own experiences, but we as outsiders can often have a more objective perspective. In this lies the genius of the Golden Rule, and if you miss it, you miss the whole point.

Philosopher Immanuel Kant criticized the Golden Rule as impractical and used the example of a criminal before a judge. If the judge practiced the Golden Rule, Kant said, then he would have to acquit all the criminals and let them go.[43] On the contrary, although it is certainly true that the criminals don't want to be incarcerated, the judge from his bird's-eye view is able to see that consequences are good for offenders and for society as a whole. So, presumably a good judge could respond to this criticism by saying, "Honestly, if I had committed a crime and come before a judge, I would want to be faced with the consequences of my actions. That way, I would see the need for repentance, be prevented from doing it again, and make the society a better place for other people to live in."

This also explains how the Rule, rightly understood, can be consistent with the seemingly harsh biblical teaching that, in some situations, we should refuse to talk to people who may want to talk to us (Matt. 7:6, Prov. 26:4). If they have proven to be closed-minded or if what you say may be used against you, it is not wise to speak and thus provide ammunition that would fuel their prejudice and slander of

Just as a treasure chest can't be unlocked with the wrong key, you won't enjoy truly good relationships if you have wrong ideas about the Golden Rule in your mind.

you. In such extreme situations, discussions about the problem never seem to achieve much, so they are rare exceptions to the normal process of loving confrontation taught by Jesus (Matt. 18:16, Luke 17:3).

Another problem with the Platinum Rule of treating others how they want to be treated is that it is so difficult to know what is in someone else's heart, and that makes it even more dangerously subjective. But let's go further…

The Golden Rule is not even about how you want to be treated. Another more subtle misunderstanding of the Rule is the idea that we should treat others as we want to be treated. As familiar as that formulation sounds, it is missing something that makes a big difference. Jesus doesn't say, "Do unto others as you want them to do unto you"; rather he says, "Do unto others as you *would* want them to do to you (if you were in their situation)." This brings an even greater measure of objectivity to the situation and encourages us to think about how we would want to be treated *if* we had a godly, biblical perspective—in other words, how we *should* want to be treated according to God's Word. That is what I believe Jesus is saying in the Golden Rule, based on its grammar and context.

This more subtle misunderstanding was illustrated by my 9-year-old daughter one Sunday when she heard me teach about the Golden Rule. She was taking

> Jesus doesn't say, "Do unto others as you want them to do unto you"; rather he says, "Do unto others as you **would** want them to do to you (if you were in their situation)."

notes by drawing pictures of what I was talking about. She drew a picture of a child asking another child for candy and getting a firm "No!" in reply! Then she drew another one, where the child says "Yes" and hands the candy over. According to her notes, the one who gave the candy was following the Golden Rule and the stingy one was not. In her mind, she was thinking, *The Golden Rule says treat people how you want*

to be treated, and when I ask for candy, I want to get it.
When she showed me her drawings, I commended her
for taking notes and for realizing that it is important
to share—but I also explained that sometimes it might
not be best to give candy to another child. Perhaps
they already had too much or perhaps their parents
had said no. "Imagine if you were the other person in
those situations," I said, "would you want someone
to give you candy?" And she answered, "I can never
imagine a situation where I wouldn't want candy!"

My daughter didn't quite get it, but hopefully you
will. What Jesus means in the Golden Rule is that you
should treat others as you would want to be treated *if
your desires were biblical and right.* This is reflected
in the KJV, NKJV, and NIV translations of Matt. 7:12
and Luke 6:31, which say "as you *would* have them
do to you" or "as you *would* want to be treated." The
NASB and ESV, on the other hand, translate both "as
you want people to treat you." I am not sure why the
NASB and ESV do that (usually they are more literal
in their renderings), because the Greek verbs in both
verses are in the subjunctive mood, which is almost
always translated as "would," or even "should."

After studying the grammar of these verses carefully, here is what I believe to be the most accurate
literal translation:

Matthew 7:12—"Whatever you would be desiring (*thelte*, present active subjunctive) that men

should do to you (*poiosin*, also subjunctive), so do to them."

Luke 6:31—"According as you are desiring (*thelete*, present active indicative) that men should do to you (*poiosin*, subjunctive), so do to them."

Jesus could have said "as you want men to do to you" without using the subjunctive mood. But since he did use the subjunctive—"would/should"—it seems he is saying "as you *would* want" (in Matthew) and "as they *should* do to you" (in both Matthew and Luke). I realize this is not conclusive evidence, because the subjunctive can have a broader meaning. But another factor makes it clear that Jesus was not saying that our own desires should be the only or final arbiter of how we treat others: the immediate and wider context of the Golden Rule.

What the Golden Rule Does Mean

The immediate context of the Golden Rule—the words surrounding it—are crucial in helping us understand it.

First, in Matthew 7:12, after Jesus states the Rule, he says, "for this is the Law and the Prophets." That means the application of the Golden Rule will never be contrary to the rest of Scripture (that's what "Law and Prophets" is referring to). What we would want people to do to us, what they *should* do to us, is defined by the rest of the Bible.

The other occurrence of the Golden Rule, in Luke 6:31, is surrounded by verses about love (vv. 27, 32, 35), and that love is clearly not defined by our feelings and desires (because we are told to love our enemies!). Love should be defined by how God says we should love, which is the way he does (vv. 35–36).

The wider context of the Golden Rule, of course, is the rest of Jesus' teachings in the Gospels plus the rest of the Bible, because it is all authoritative revelation from him (2 Tim. 3:16–17, 2 Pet. 1:20–21). That is why we can't just allow our desires or the desires of others to be the decisive factor in our actions toward them. We must consider what *should be done* according to Scripture, not just what we *want* to be done.

In the introduction to this book, I mentioned a sermon by Rev. James Forbes, pastor and professor at Union Seminary in New York, who admitted to having trouble finding the Golden Rule in his Bible. In that message, Forbes says that the Golden Rule led him to tell a man dying of AIDS that God accepted him and affirmed his gay lifestyle.[44] Although I believe the Golden Rule should cause us to treat all people with love and respect, and even to empathize with their feelings and preferences, it cannot possibly mean that we must condone behavior that the Bible says is wrong (Rom. 1:26–27, 1 Cor. 6:9–11). The proper application of the Golden Rule in that case would be to tell the man that he needs to repent and seek forgiveness—because if *we* were separated from God and headed for judgment, we would want to know. But it should also be done in a loving and caring way, of course, since that is

> Liberal theologian Paul Tillich said, "the problem with the rule is that it does not tell us what we should wish." But, in answer to this, the rest of Scripture does.

the way we would want to be treated in the same situation. (I always tell my LGBTQ friends that my sins are just as bad or worse than theirs are, and that we both need forgiveness and change.)

This is the answer to the two criticisms of the Golden Rule that I mentioned in Chapter One—one serious and one not so serious. I'll repeat them here briefly. First, liberal theologian Paul Tillich said, "the problem with the rule is that it does not tell us what we *should* wish."[45] But, in answer to this, the rest of Scripture does. And secondly, George Bernard Shaw quipped, "Don't do to others as you want them to do to you. Their tastes may be different."[46] But when you understand the Golden Rule as Jesus meant it, you will understand that our "tastes" must be evaluated by the "Law and Prophets" and the "law of love," to see whether they really are best for us or not.

Perhaps the best historical definition and explanation of the Golden Rule can be found in the writings of the English philosopher and theologian Samuel Clarke (1675–1729):

> Whatever I judge reasonable or unreasonable for another to do for me; that, by the same judgement, I declare reasonable or unreasonable, that I in the like case should do for him.[47]

That is a good definition, as long as our standard for what is reasonable or unreasonable is the Word of God, since all sound reason comes from God. Clarke also takes on Kant's criticism about criminals and a judge (and whether the judge should simply let all criminals go, because that is what they would like), in the following helpful passage:

> For example, a magistrate, in order to deal equitably with a criminal, is not to consider what fear or *self-love* would cause him, in the criminal's case, to desire; but what reason and the public good would oblige him to acknowledge was fit and just for him to *expect*. And the same proportion is to be observed, in deducing the duties of parents and children, of masters and servants, of governors and subjects, of citizens and foreigners.[48]

Jeffrey Wattles' explanation of the essence of the Golden Rule takes the form of a logical tautology:

1. Treat others as *you* want others to treat you.

2. You want others to treat you with appropriate sympathy, respect, and so on.

3. Therefore, treat others with appropriate sympathy, respect, and so on.

… Notice that our sense of what is *appropriate* represents an estimate of *value*.[49]

The values we find in the rest of Scripture enable us to apply the Golden Rule in the right way. So perhaps the best definition of the Golden Rule is this:

Treat others as you would want to be treated if you were in their situation, doing what is best for them according to the principles of Scripture.

The next chapter will take what we have learned about the meaning of the Rule and guide us through a step-by-step process of applying it, illustrated by a practical, everyday situation.

Questions for Thought and Discussion

1. The versions of the Golden Rule prior to Christ were almost all stated negatively, but he established its use in the positive form. Why did he do that?

2. The Golden Rule is not "treat others as they want to be treated," but "treat others as *you* would want to be treated." What is the difference between the two?

3. *My daughter misunderstood the Golden Rule when she thought that she should always give candy to her friend, because she couldn't imagine a situation where she wouldn't want candy. What was missing in her thinking?*

4. *A good definition of the Golden Rule is, "Treat others as you would want to be treated if you were in their situation, doing what is best for them **according to the principles of Scripture**." Why is the last part of that definition so important?*

four

FASHIONED

Applying the Golden Rule in Everyday Life

Charles Spurgeon spoke the following words about 150 years ago, and they are still true today.

> Everything that has gone before leads up to this.... In this place our King gives us his golden rule. Put yourself in another's place and then act to him as you would wish him to act towards you under the same circumstances. This is a right royal rule, a precept always at hand, always applicable, always right. Here you may be a judge, and yet not be judging others, but judging for others. This is the sum of the Decalogue, the Pentateuch, and the whole sacred Word. Oh, that all men acted on it and then there would be no slavery, no war, no sweating, no striking, no lying, no robbing, but all would be justice and love![50]

Since the Golden Rule is "always applicable, always right," we need to know how to use this key to unlock the treasure of blessed relationships. So the following eight steps provide a guide for practicing the Golden Rule in any situation or decision. Each step will be illustrated by the following scenario, one that someone asked me about while I was working on this book:

- You've noticed some bad behavior by a child in the church, which seems to have gone unaddressed by his parents on numerous occasions. You've thought about talking to the parents about this, but you don't know them very well and you're afraid that would cause an uncomfortable rift between you and them. What should you do?

Step One
Think About the Other Person's Situation

The Golden Rule says that you should treat others as you would want to be treated if you were that person. To do that, you must begin by thinking about their situation. Philippians 2:3–4 teaches this idea:

Do nothing from selfish ambition or conceit, but in humility count others more significant than yourselves. Let each of you look not only to his own interests, but also to the interests of others.

After telling us that we should not be selfish but

rather other-person-centered in all our relationships, the apostle Paul helps us with *how* to do that by saying we should look out for the interests of others. He means that we should think about others as much or more as we do about ourselves, and by doing so, we will become more humble and selfless. To think rightly about the situation of others, we need to listen and learn, rather than making rash judgments. As Jesus said, "Do not judge by the outward appearance, but judge with righteous judgment" (John 7:24). We need to spend more time with our ears open and our mouths shut. We need to be "quick to hear, slow to speak," as James 1:19 says. Consider also these verses from Proverbs 18, which could be called "the listening chapter":

> A fool takes no pleasure in understanding, but only in expressing his opinion. (v. 2)

> If one gives an answer before he hears, it is his folly and shame. (v. 13)

> The one who states his case first seems right, until the other comes and examines him. (v. 17)

If we put our minds in gear and our mouths in Neutral (or better yet, in Park), we will be well on our way to practicing the Golden Rule. We should learn about the others involved in a problem, and carefully consider what we learn about them. In the situation with the badly behaved child, for example, do you really know what is going on? How about talking to the parents first, showing an interest in them, asking them questions about themselves and their situation before proceeding further? Maybe it will be appropriate to talk to other people about the couple, and about their child (although to avoid gossip, you should try to do this without saying negative things about any of them). Are they new believers who are not as far along as you in their spiritual journey? Are they non-believers with a different worldview? Has the family experienced difficulties you were previously unaware of? How

We should think about others as much or more as we do about ourselves, and by doing so, we will become more humble and selfless.

much do you understand their circumstances—their home, their work situation, their wider family? Do you know if the child has been through any particular difficulties in his young life? Does he have any special needs, such as autism? Think about how they are they are likely to react if you talk to them about this. Has anyone else already talked to them, about this or other related issues? Get as much information as you can, *think about them*—and pray for them as you do—rather than just relying on your own initial observations, parental preferences, or hasty conclusions.

Step Two

Imagine Yourself In Their Shoes

After you think about the other person's situation, you must then imagine yourself in it. In order to treat others as you would want to be treated if you were "in their shoes," you have to "put yourself in their shoes" and visualize what it would be like to be them. I mentioned earlier that forms of the Golden Rule are found in many cultural and religious traditions throughout the world, and that includes Native Americans. The Sioux had a prayer that captures this idea well: "Great Spirit, grant that I may not criticize my neighbor until I have walked a mile in his moccasins."[51]

The greatest example of this principle, as you might guess, is the Lord Jesus Christ. He embodies the Golden Rule in everything he does, and in his incarnation, he literally embodied this particular step of putting himself in our shoes. Hebrews 2:17–18 says,

> He had to be made like his brothers in every respect, so that he might become a merciful and faithful high priest in the service of God, to make propitiation for the sins of the people. For because he himself has suffered when tempted, he is able to help those who are being tempted.

The amazing truth that we celebrate at Christmas is that Jesus Christ did not only imagine himself in our place, he actually *put himself in our place*, becoming one of us! He left a heavenly throne where he had been worshipped eternally as God himself, and came down to a hay-filled trough to live a life of ignominy and pain as a human being. And we are called to emulate his love and humility in our relationships with others (John 13:34; Phil. 2:5–8).

Later in Hebrews, the writer mentions our Lord's understanding about the situation of others. Hebrews 4:15 puts it like this: "We do not have a high priest who is unable to sympathize with our weaknesses, but one who in every respect has been tempted as we are, yet without sin." To sympathize means to "feel with" or "feel together"—Jesus knows what it is like to be in our situation! And through his Golden Rule, he calls us to do that same thing to others, because to treat others as you would want to be treated, you must imagine what it is like to be in their situation. This is even more than imagining yourself in their situation… you must imagine what it is like to be *that person*, to put yourself in *his or her shoes.* Then you will begin to gain the understanding you need to apply the Golden Rule. You need to get "outside of yourself" as much as you can.

Speaking of Christmas, one of the most beloved pieces of holiday entertainment illustrates this principle well. In Charles Dickens' *A Christmas Carol,* Ebenezer Scrooge is a selfish man who does not live by the Golden Rule, to say the least. He has no compassion or kindness and treats others with contempt and rudeness. But he is visited on Christmas Eve by three "spirits," one of whom takes him to the home of one of the people he has mistreated—his clerk, Bob Cratchit. There, like an unwilling fly on the wall, Scrooge is forced to watch the Cratchit family. He begins to understand them better as he witnesses their hopes, dreams, fears, and deprivations—even their feelings about him! Scrooge can now see for the first time what life is like for these people, and even imagine himself in their shoes. He starts to mellow and become more caring and compassionate toward them, as they become *people* to him, rather than mere objects. This

> *To treat others as you would want to be treated, you must imagine what it is like to be in their situation.*

is a significant turning point in his character and in the story, which ends with Scrooge attending church for the first time in many years and beginning a new life of Golden Rule living.[52]

In the illustration of the parents at church whose child is behaving badly, how can you apply this step of imagining yourself in their shoes? If the parents have not known the Lord as long as you have, you could think back to when you were younger in the Lord, and how little you knew about God's ways and how to walk in them. You could think of your own children, if you have them, and think of time when you or they had problems, and what things were like for you then. Imagine *yourself* struggling with ignorance and negligence (as you have many times, I'm sure). Think of a time when you felt judged or criticized by someone. Can you remember how you felt—what was it like? Try to imagine the thoughts, feelings, hopes, and dreams the child's parents must be experiencing right now, as well as all the disappointments, failures, and sins. You will then be ready for the next step.

Step Three
Think about How You Would Want to be Treated

Now, after first thinking about their situation and then imagining yourself in their shoes, the next step is to think about what is best for them—or what would be best for you *if you were them*. Notice the emphasis on *thinking* in the first three steps of applying the Golden Rule… this is where it all starts—in our minds. In fact, that is not only true of the Golden Rule, but of all other aspects of Christian living. At the beginning of Romans 12, after spending eleven chapters discussing the great doctrines of the gospel (what God has done for us), Paul then turns to address the moral and practical response we should have to those great truths (what we should do for God). And he summarizes the whole Christian life in this way, in verses 1 and 2:

> I appeal to you therefore, brothers, by the mercies of God, to present your bodies as a living sacrifice, holy and acceptable to God, which is your spiritual worship. Do not be conformed to this world, but be transformed by the renewal of your mind, that by testing you may discern what is the will of God, what is good and acceptable and perfect.

Once we have committed ourselves to pleasing God with our lives, because of the great mercies he has bestowed upon us in Christ, the primary way that we grow in him and the foundation for all our service to him is *the renewing of our minds*. Everything starts there, and everything flows from there. Proverbs 4:23 says, "Keep your heart with all vigilance, for from it flow the springs of life." Paul teaches the same idea in 2 Corinthians 10:3–5:

> For though we walk in the flesh, we are not waging war according to the flesh. For the weapons of our warfare are not of the flesh but have divine power to destroy strongholds. We destroy arguments and every lofty opinion raised against the knowledge of God, and take every thought captive to obey Christ.

At its most fundamental level, spiritual warfare is fought in our minds, at the level of *what we think about*. That is why the first three steps of applying the

Golden Rule have to do with our thoughts, and that is why we can't begin to act in a loving way toward someone until we first think about how we would want to be treated in that situation, and what is best for them. So you might say that, when it comes to practicing the Golden Rule, the way we think is the key to the key.

The application of this step may seem fairly obvious: I wouldn't want to be abused, so I shouldn't abuse others; I wouldn't want to be robbed, so I shouldn't steal; I wouldn't want to be deceived, so I shouldn't lie; etc. But in other situations the answer may not be so

> *At its most fundamental level, spiritual warfare is fought in our minds, at the level of what we think about.*

clear. For example, in our scenario about the parents with a misbehaving child, you might have some difficulty when you ask yourself, *How would I want to be treated if my child was bothering people?* You might think, *I'm not sure I would want to be told about that, because that would be painful to hear, and it would mean a lot of work on my part to address it, and it may strain the relationship between me and the people who tell me,* etc. Because our thinking is not always totally clear, or may even be wrong, it becomes necessary to proceed to the next step.

Step Four

Compare Your Thoughts to Scripture

Think about the others' situation, imagine yourself in their shoes, think about how you would want to be treated—then compare those thoughts to Scripture. We need to ask ourselves, *What does the Bible say about it?*

As we have learned in the previous chapters, the rest of Scripture provides the necessary context for understanding and applying the Golden Rule rightly. The whole Word of God supplies the value system that tells us what is really best for others, and what we *should* want if we were in their situation. Divorcing the Golden Rule from the rest of God's truth is what has led to its misuse and abuse throughout history, and even to the decline of its reputation in recent years in our culture. We must make sure to understand it in its context and connect it with the other biblical principles that apply to the situation.

We must be careful not to assume the rightness of our initial thoughts when we think, *What would I want to be done to me?* We need to compare those thoughts to Scripture, and consider questions like:

- What does the Bible say?

- What are God's goals for this situation and what, therefore, should my goals be?

- What does God want to happen here, and what is most important to him according to his Word?
- What does God say is best for this other person, and for me?

The Scriptures are given to us to tell us what is best for us, as God says to Israel in Joshua 1:7–8:

> Only be strong and very courageous, being careful to do according to all the law that Moses my servant commanded you. Do not turn from it to the right hand or to the left, that you may have good success wherever you go. This Book of the Law shall not depart from your mouth, but you shall meditate on it day and night, so that you may be careful to do according to all that is written in it. For then you will make your way prosperous, and then you will have good success.

When we follow the Word of God, that not only brings glory to God, it also brings good to us. But if we ignore or disregard the teaching of Scripture, we can have no hope of spiritual success. Consider the following verses:

> And the Lord will make you abound in prosperity… if you obey the commandments of the Lord your God, which I command you today, being careful to do them, and if you do not turn aside from any of the words that I command you today,

to the right hand or to the left, to go after other gods to serve them. But if you will not obey the voice of the Lord your God or be careful to do all his commandments and his statutes that I command you today, then all these curses shall come upon you and overtake you. Cursed shall you be in the city, and cursed shall you be in the field. Cursed shall be your basket and your kneading bowl. Cursed shall be the fruit of your womb and the fruit of your ground, the increase of your herds and the young of your flock. Cursed shall you be when you come in, and cursed shall you be when you go out. (Deut. 28:11–19)

Blessed is the man who walks not in the counsel of the wicked, nor stands in the way of sinners, nor sits in the seat of scoffers; but his delight is in the law of the Lord, and on his law he meditates day and night.

He is like a tree planted by streams of water that yields its fruit in its season, and its leaf does not wither. In all that he does, he prospers. The wicked are not so, but are like chaff that the wind drives away. (Psa. 1:1–4)

If your law had not been my delight, I would have perished in my affliction. I will never forget your precepts, for by them you have given me life. (Psa. 119:92–93)

Therefore put away all filthiness and rampant wickedness and receive with meekness the implanted word, which is able to save your souls. But be doers of the word, and not hearers only, deceiving yourselves. For if anyone is a hearer of the word and not a doer, he is like a man who looks intently at his natural face in a mirror. For he looks at himself and goes away and at once forgets what he was like. But the one who looks into the perfect law, the law of liberty, and perseveres, being no hearer who forgets but a doer who acts, he will be blessed in his doing. (James 1:21–25)

Since knowing and doing what the Bible says is the key to spiritual success in all aspects of life, we need to understand and follow it when we seek to apply Christ's key to relationships. In this step, counsel from others becomes very important, because we may not know all that the Bible says about the situation and we may need help from others who know more than we do. The book of Proverbs says:

Whoever trusts in his own mind is a fool (28:26)

The way of a fool is right in his own eyes, but a wise man listens to advice. (12:15)

By insolence comes nothing but strife, but with those who take advice is wisdom. (13:10)

Without counsel plans fail, but with many advisers they succeed (15:22)

> Listen to advice and accept instruction, that you
> may gain wisdom in the future (19:20)

During this step of comparing your thoughts to Scripture, make sure that you ask for any help you need from others, testing out your assumptions before continuing with the process.

In our scenario of the troubled child with troubled parents, here's how this step should go: If you think, *I wouldn't want someone to tell me about problems with my child*, think again in light of what the Word of God says. In Scripture, we see all those verses about true success coming from following God and good counsel, so we should *want* others to help us see how we are not living by the Word. What's more, the Bible specifically talks about the blessing of confrontation

> Since knowing and doing what the Bible says is the key to spiritual success in all aspects of life, we need to understand and follow it when we seek to apply Christ's key to relationships.

or rebuke when we need it—although none of us relishes the prospect! Psalm 141:5 says, "Let a righteous man strike me—it is a kindness; let him rebuke me—it is oil for my head," and Proverbs 27:5–6 says, "Better is open rebuke than hidden love. Faithful are the wounds of a friend."

When we think about God's goals for this situation, and therefore what our goals *should be* for this situation, and then combine that with the principles of loving correction, the best thing to do would probably be to talk to the parents about their child's behavior. After all, these parents *should* be wanting to honor God, and to be helping their child to honor God, so they *should* want others to help them toward that goal. Honoring God *should* be more important than any bad feelings or awkward interaction that might result from such a loving intervention. Also relevant to the situation would be Scriptures about the good results of raising children the right way (Prov. 22:6, 15; Eph. 6:1–4) and the bad results of not doing so (1 Sam. 3:13; Prov. 29:15).

But notice that the Scripture also says, "Faithful are the wounds of a friend." It is vital that this discussion takes place in the context of friendship rather than a businesslike or holier-than-thou interaction. And other scriptural principles may apply, like the priority of the marriage relationship over even our relationship with children, and the need and benefits of community in the process of spiritual growth. We will talk about those more later in this chapter, but for now let's go on to the next step in applying the Golden Rule.

Step Five
Recognize and Confess Your Sin

As you understand the others' situation, and then think about how you would want to be treated if you were in their shoes and compare those thoughts to Scripture, you will usually be convicted of your own sin by the Holy Spirit. That will happen because the Golden Rule summarizes the essence of the law of God. And, as we discussed earlier, the primary purpose of the law of God is to show us our sin, so that we might see our need for Christ (Rom. 3:19–20, Gal. 3:21–24). So, any attempt to practice the Golden Rule will reveal our sin in one way or another, which it is designed by God to do.

Consider how this could happen in the situation of the misbehaving child in the church. As you think about the Golden Rule and try to apply it, you may realize any number of ways that your own heart and life are not in line with God's will for you. First, you may simply realize that you do not know what to do in the situation; you are too ignorant of the Word of God to know how it applies. Or, if you do know what is best to do, you may not *want* to do what is best. Particularly if you realize you should confront the parents about the child's behavior, you probably won't want to do that, even though you may think it's best for them (most people don't like to confront others). Your sin may be what the Bible calls fear of man (Prov. 29:25), which is really pride and idolatry (caring more about what people think of us than what God thinks of us). You may be too busy or lazy to do anything about it, which is the sin of selfishness. You may be unwilling to befriend the family in order to help them with their problems, which is pride *and* selfishness! You may not

> *The gospel of Christ will mean more to us when we take the time to recognize our own sinfulness and need for God's grace.*

want to expose yourself to scrutiny (*What if they start telling me what's wrong with **my** kids?*), and you may not be willing to spend the time and energy it might take to deal with the situation in the right way. Finally, as you think about their situation, you may remember all the times that you yourself have sinned in similar ways in the past.

If any of these problems in your own life become apparent to you in this process, confess them to God. The first reason to do so is simply because it is the right thing to do:

> Whoever conceals his transgressions will not prosper, but he who confesses and forsakes them will obtain mercy. (Prov. 28:13)

> Blessed is the man against whom the Lord counts no iniquity, and in whose spirit there is no deceit.

For when I kept silent, my bones wasted away through my groaning all day long. For day and night your hand was heavy upon me; my strength was dried up as by the heat of summer. *Selah*

I acknowledged my sin to you, and I did not cover my iniquity; I said, "I will confess my transgressions to the Lord," and you forgave the iniquity of my sin. (Psa. 32:2–5)

If we say we have no sin, we deceive ourselves, and the truth is not in us. If we confess our sins, he is faithful and just to forgive us our sins and to cleanse us from all unrighteousness. (1 John 1:8–9)

Another reason to confess the sin that God reveals to us is that it will help us with the next steps in the process. The gospel of Christ will mean more to us when we take the time to recognize our own sinfulness and need for God's grace. The humility this produces will in turn prepare us to act in a gracious way toward others.

Step Six
Repent and Believe the Gospel

You may have heard Christians talk about the idea of "living in the gospel" rather than just being saved by it, or the fact that "the gospel is for Christians, too." Living a "gospel-centered life" and "preaching the gospel

to yourself" have become catch-phrases among believers steeped in the grace of God and the doctrine
of Divine Sonship.[53] The truth reflected in these ex-
pressions is summarized by Colossians 2:6–7: "*As you
received Christ Jesus the Lord, so walk in him, rooted
and built up in him and established in the faith, just as
you were taught, abounding in thanksgiving.*"

In that passage, the apostle Paul says the way in
which we receive Christ (by grace through faith) is
the same way we are to continue to grow in him (by
grace through faith). And this applies to our practice
of the Golden Rule, as well as every other aspect of the
Christian life. In fact, this step of the process will help
us to understand how the idea of "living by the gospel"
works in a practical, everyday situation.

When you try to apply the Golden Rule to a situation like the misbehaving child, and you become aware
of your sins of ignorance, fear of man, pride, or selfishness, allow this realization to "send you to Jesus" in
your heart. *Recognize* your sin ("I am wrong"), *repent*
from it ("I'm sorry, Lord, please forgive and change
me") and *remember* what Christ has done for you
("Thank you, Jesus, for dying for my sins so that I can
be forgiven, and thank you for rising from the dead
so I can be changed!"). Find your assurance, identity,
and joy in the gospel truth that God does not relate to
you on the basis of your performance, but on the basis
of the righteousness of Christ, freely given to us as we

trust in him. Take courage and hope from the wonderful promise that God is no longer angry and wrathful toward you, because Christ has appeased his wrath through his substitutionary sacrifice on the cross. He died for all your sins, including the sins of ignorance, pride, and selfishness! As you reflect on that sacrifice and thank him for it, you can rejoice that the penalty for sin has been removed. As Romans 6:11 says, "Consider yourselves dead to sin and alive to God in Christ Jesus."

As we reflect not only on the cross but on the empty tomb, we can also rejoice that the *power* of sin has been broken, and that we are now "alive to God in Christ Jesus." Because Jesus is alive and has sent his Spirit into our lives, we can really change by his power! We don't have to be so ignorant, proud, and selfish anymore—we can "rid [ourselves] of the old self, which is being corrupted in accordance with the lusts of deceit... and put on the new self, which in the likeness of God has been created in righteousness and holiness of the truth" (Eph. 4:22–24).

In this way, by "re-visiting" the cross and the empty tomb in our hearts, we will be repenting of our sins and believing the gospel, and we will be prepared to continue applying the Golden Rule in the only way that truly pleases God and makes a difference for his kingdom. We will be practicing it because of grace rather than "dead works" (Heb. 6:1, 9:14) and we will be doing it out of gratitude to God instead of a vain attempt to earn his love and favor. We also will be able to give God all the glory for any good we do, knowing it was only by his grace, rather than becoming proud and self-righteous because we think we are somehow better than others. And finally, we will be able to take decisive action on the crucial next step without a debilitating fear of failure, because we will know that God will love us even if we don't get everything right. We can do our best with the confidence that if we get it wrong somehow, he will forgive us in Christ and work everything together for good (Rom. 8:28). All these are benefits of living a gospel-centered life.

Step Seven
Do for Them What Would Be Best for You

After you have thought about the other person's situation, imagined yourself in their shoes, considered how you would want to be treated, compared your own thoughts to Scripture, confessed your own sin, and repented and remembered the gospel, then you should do for others what you would want done to you. Now is the time to take action—to serve and help them in the best way you can, being motivated to obey the Lord's command by his goodness and grace to us. Although thinking is an essential part of applying the Golden Rule, as we have seen, *thinking by itself* will never fulfill Jesus' intention in giving it to us. We must turn our thoughts into action.

To help illustrate what "Golden Rule action" is like in a concrete and specific way, let me explain what I would do in the situation of the misbehaving child.

First, if the parents are clearly believers in Christ, I would make a firm decision in my mind that, before too long, I will talk to them about the problem. They need to know there is a problem, and they probably need help with it. If I were in their position, I would want others to tell me if they thought my child was out of control. I want to do the best job I can as a parent,

> *Although thinking is an essential part of applying the Golden Rule, as we have seen, thinking alone will never fulfill Jesus' intention in giving it to us. We must turn our thoughts into action.*

and I realize that I may be blind to areas of weakness that need to be addressed. Often, the only way to discover these areas is to hear from others who are more objective and can see things I do not. Also, my relationship to the parents and their child is not likely to improve if I don't address the issue. In fact, those relationships will probably worsen. So, for these reasons and more, I would commit myself to talking to them about the problem, because it's the right thing to do. If

I am not sure how to address it with them, I will begin praying about it and seeking some counsel from others, without mentioning any names.

Before I actually talk to them, however, I would first try to develop more of a relationship with them. Remember that the original account of the scenario said, "you don't know them very well and you are afraid that would cause an uncomfortable rift between you and them." Proverbs 27:6 says, "Faithful are the wounds of a friend," so I would find some ways to establish a genuine friendship, before the faithful wounds of hearing that their child's behavior is a prob-

After showing us by his incarnation that he was our friend and that he loved us, Jesus took the action that was necessary to meet our needs, to do what was best for us.

lem. Perhaps I would invite them over for dinner, join in a church ministry in which they are involved, find some common interest, or just talk with them more often when I have the chance. But I would make a strategic effort to know them better—never wavering in my commitment to confront the situation but wanting to do it in a way that could have the best results possible. I also might try to learn more about their marriage first, before addressing the issue of the child, because many times problems with children are a reflection of problems between the mother and father. If they are open about such difficulties, that would give me the opportunity to encourage them and find the best way of helping them with that primary relationship.

If the couple are not believers, however, I would take a different approach. My goal would be to talk to them about the gospel, not their child's behavior. I would not expect the child to be behaving well when the power of the Holy Spirit is not yet at work in their home. What they need most at this point is to get to know Christ personally. Once they have done that, other parts of their lives will inevitably begin to change, including the way they raise their children. At some point, while I am sharing the gospel with them, I may mention some issue related to the child, but that would only be for the purpose of helping them to see why they need Christ and how he can meet the needs in their lives. Maybe they do feel bad about their child's behavior, and I could use that as a way to show them the hope that is in Christ. It should go without saying that I would also be building a relationship of friendship with them as best as I can, because that can only help in the process of evangelism and discipleship.

This will all take time and energy—but I hope, by God's grace, that I would see this as an opportunity he has granted me to serve him. I realize that someone might be thinking, *What if this relationship with the family endangers you or your own family in some way?* Although we should be wise and perhaps establish some boundaries in the relationship, we also must realize that there is always some risk involved in kingdom work (the ministry of the apostle Paul shows us that). I would view any wrong behavior of the child, or the parents for that matter, as an opportunity to teach my children and pray with them about it, involving them in the ministry of making disciples so that they can learn what it means to fulfill the Great Commission of Christ (Matt. 28:19–20).

Once again, Jesus himself is the ultimate example of this step of applying the Golden Rule. He willingly gave up his time, energy, security and even his life to do what was best for us, and to make us his disciples. Philippians 2:5–8 says:

> Have this mind among yourselves, which is yours in Christ Jesus, who, though he was in the form of God, did not count equality with God a thing to be grasped, but emptied himself, by taking the form of a servant, being born in the likeness of men. And being found in human form, he humbled himself by becoming obedient to the point of death, even death on a cross.

After showing us by his incarnation that he was our friend and that he loved us, Jesus took the action that was necessary to meet our needs, to do what was best for us. And in verses 9–11, we see the results of his loving action, and are led into our final step in applying the Golden Rule:

Therefore God has highly exalted him and bestowed on him the name that is above every name, so that at the name of Jesus every knee should bow, in heaven and on earth and under the earth, and every tongue confess that Jesus Christ is Lord, to the glory of God the Father.

Step Eight
Give the Glory to God!

When you have obeyed the Golden Rule and done what you believe is best for others, you must make sure to give God the glory for anything good you have done. As 1 Corinthians 10:31 says, "Whatever you do, do all to the glory of God." Imagine yourself one more time in the scenario of the "problem child," and you will see how this step is applied.

First, give the glory to God if you are *praised*. Suppose you follow the Golden Rule as I have suggested, and the parents say to you, "Thank you so much. That took a lot of guts to talk to us about that, and we really admire you for it." Say to them, or at least in your heart, "All glory to God." Don't fail to give him the glory. Don't be like King Herod in Acts 12:21–23:

On an appointed day Herod put on his royal robes, took his seat upon the throne, and delivered an oration to them. And the people were shouting, "The voice of a god, and not of a man!"

> Immediately an angel of the Lord struck him down, because he did not give God the glory, and he was eaten by worms and breathed his last.

Do you know what it means that King Herod was "eaten by worms"? Neither do I, but I know it was really bad! And it happened to him simply because he failed to give God the glory when he was being praised. He did not even brag and say, "Yeah, I *am* great, aren't I?!" His silence alone was enough to condemn him to that dreadful death. So, if your application of the Golden Rule is met with appreciation, be sure to give credit where credit is due.

The ultimate reason for practicing the Golden Rule is to glorify God. That makes it worthwhile, regardless of what kind of response or results we may experience.

Second, give the glory to God not only if you are praised, but also if you are *persecuted*. The parents in this scenario may say to you, "Who do you think you are to talk to us about our child? This is none of your business, you self-righteous Pharisee! Let me tell you about *your* kids…" If they do respond this way, or with some other form of hostility, then give God the glory in that situation as well! Consider these words from 1 Peter 4:12–16:

> Beloved, do not be surprised at the fiery trial when it comes upon you to test you, as though something strange were happening to you. But rejoice insofar as you share Christ's sufferings, that you may also rejoice and be glad when his glory is revealed. If you are insulted for the name of Christ, you are blessed, because the Spirit of glory and of God rests upon you. But let none of you suffer as a murderer or a thief or an evildoer or as a meddler. Yet if anyone suffers as a Christian, let him not be ashamed, but let him glorify God in that name.

The ultimate reason for practicing the Golden Rule is to glorify God. That makes it worthwhile, regardless of what kind of response or results we may experience. But we do believe, along with Charles Spurgeon, that a faithful application of the Rule will indeed bear great fruit, in God's timing and by his power:

> What a kingdom is this which has such a law! This is the condensation of all that is right and generous. We adore the King out of whose mouth and heart such a law could flow. This one rule is a proof of the divinity of our holy religion. The universal practice of it by all who call themselves Christians would carry conviction to Jew, Turk, and infidel, with greater speed and certainty than all the apologies and arguments which the wit or piety of men could produce.

Lord, teach it to me! Write it on the fleshly tablets of my renewed heart! Write it out in full in my life![54]

Questions for Thought and Discussion

1. To apply the Golden Rule, you must first think about the other person's situation, what it would be like to be in their shoes, and how you would want to be treated if you were. Why is your thinking so important and foundational to this process?

2. After you think about how you would want to be treated, you should compare your thoughts to Scripture. Why is this so important?

3. Before you put the Golden Rule into action in a particular situation, you should first "preach the gospel to yourself." What does that mean and why does it matter?

4. You can apply this practical process to any relationship challenge you may experience. Think of a recent or current problem in your life and apply the steps in this chapter by walking through them in your mind and applying them to the situation.

five

DO UNTO OTHERS

You Hold the Key

The Golden Rule should be constantly on the lips and in the hearts of God's people. We should often be asking ourselves, *How can I treat this person as I would want to be treated?* And we should regularly be encouraging others by saying to them, "How would the Golden Rule apply in this situation?"

A case could be made that questions like these are even better than the more famous slogan, "What would Jesus do?" Of course, we should definitely seek to be like Christ (Rom. 8:29, 1 Cor. 11:1), but there are some things about him that we will never be able to emulate—like his divine attributes and authority. The Golden Rule, however, is a saying that Jesus himself spoke, and said to us directly, with the intention that we should live by it in all circumstances.

The context of the two times Christ spoke the Golden Rule in the Gospels shows us how important it is for our salvation, our spiritual growth, and our service to others. Matthew 7:12, for example, is the concluding statement for the largest section of the Sermon on the Mount. The verse says, "In everything, *therefore*, treat people the same way you want them to treat you, for this is the Law and the Prophets." The word *therefore* is "there for" the purpose of indicating that Jesus is summarizing everything he has said in the entire sermon.

Martin Luther pointed this out in the sixteenth century when he wrote:

> With those words He concludes the instructions contained in those three chapters, and gathers them all into one little bundle.[55]

In the eighteenth century, English Baptist pastor John Gill commented:

> These words are the epilogue, or conclusion of our Lord's discourse; the sum of what he had delivered in the two preceding chapters, and in this hitherto, is contained in these words.[56]

And in the nineteenth century, German commentator H. A. W. Meyer said:

> At this point Jesus takes a retrospective glance at all that He has been saying since Matthew 5:17,—beginning with Moses and the prophets,—concerning our duty to our neighbour, but introducing, indeed, many other instructions and exhortations. But putting out of view such

matters as are foreign to His discourse, He now recapitulates all that has been said on the duties we owe to our neighbour, so that ["therefore"] points back to Matthew 5:17.[57]

The fact that Jesus calls for a response in the very next verse ("Enter through the narrow gate") is one of the reasons we should view the Golden Rule statement in Matthew 7:12 as a summary of the whole previous section, in which he explained and applied the Old Testament law so that his audience would realize their sinfulness and need for a Savior. This also shows how the Rule can be effective in evangelism. Many outreach models—like Evangelism Explosion and Way of the Master—use questions like "Have you ever lied?" (from the Ten Commandments) and "Have you ever lusted?" (from the Sermon on the Mount) to help people realize that we "all have sinned and fall short of the glory of God" (Rom. 3:23). Given Jesus' words here in Matthew 7, we can conclude that an equally appropriate question would be, "Do you always treat others as you would want them to treat you?"

Perhaps you yourself are recognizing that you have fallen far short of God's perfect standard for your relationships. If so, I want to encourage you to hear and obey the words that Jesus spoke right after he quoted the Golden Rule:

> Enter by the narrow gate. For the gate is wide and the way is easy that leads to destruction, and

those who enter by it are many. For the gate is narrow and the way is hard that leads to life, and those who find it are few. (Matt. 7:13–14)

Come right now to the Savior who offers you eternal life in heaven and a changed life here! Don't let family or peer pressure keep you from starting (and staying) on his path through repentance from sin and faith in what he has done for us. He died on the cross, paying the penalty for sin, so you could be forgiven for all of yours. And he rose from the dead so you could live the way he wants you to, which is also the way that is best for you.

In case you still don't fully see why you need forgiveness and change in Christ, consider the context of the other time the Golden Rule is quoted in the Bible.

> *Jesus died on the cross, paying the penalty for sin, so you could be forgiven for all of yours. And he rose from the dead so you could live the way he wants you to, which is also the way that is best for you.*

Luke 6:31 is surrounded by specific applications of the principle, which will not allow us to say something like, "Oh, I think I treat others pretty well." Notice the incredibly high standard Jesus establishes in this passage, and how we all fail to live up to it in the many situations he mentions:

But I say to you who hear, Love your enemies, do good to those who hate you, bless those who curse you, pray for those who abuse you. To one who strikes you on the cheek, offer the other also, and from one who takes away your cloak do not withhold your tunic either. Give to everyone who begs from you, and from one who takes away your goods do not demand them back. And as you wish that others would do to you, do so to them.

If you love those who love you, what benefit is that to you? For even sinners love those who love them. And if you do good to those who do good to you, what benefit is that to you? For even sinners do the same. And if you lend to those from whom you expect to receive, what credit is that to you? Even sinners lend to sinners, to get back the same amount. But love your enemies, and do good, and lend, expecting nothing in return, and your reward will be great, and you will be sons of the Most High, for he is kind to the ungrateful and the evil. Be merciful, even as your Father is merciful.

Judge not, and you will not be judged; condemn not, and you will not be condemned; forgive, and you will be forgiven; give, and it will be given to you. Good measure, pressed down, shaken together, running over, will be put into your lap.

> For with the measure you use it will be measured
> back to you. (Luke 6:27–38)

What human being, besides Christ himself, has ever kept all the requirements in that passage, or even come close? Not me, not you, not anyone! Take the command, for example, which says, "Give to everyone who asks of you." Certainly, we need to practice that command with the teaching of the rest of Scripture in mind, and not contradict other principles in the Word.

- So regarding the man in the illustration I mentioned in Chapter One, who a second time asks you for money to help pay his bills but doesn't want to have any financial advice, he may not be best served by giving him what he is asking for in that particular situation. It might not be good for him, and the attempt to help him may actually hurt him.[58]

But, in most other cases, when there is no clear indication of a problem like that, you should "give to everyone who asks of you."

- So if a woman in the subway asks you to buy her a train ticket so she can get home, you should do it. (I don't suggest giving her cash that she could spend in some other way, of course, but a ticket seems to be a very legitimate need in that case.)

When we add in all the times that people have asked for help when they're moving, and other needs that we have been less than eager to meet, you can see how the standard of the law is so high that Jesus would say, "unless your righteousness far surpasses that of the scribes and Pharisees, you will not enter the kingdom of heaven" (Matt. 5:20). Not to mention all the times we have not loved our enemies and prayed for those who mistreat us, how many people we have judged unfairly when we didn't have enough information to really know the situation, and the money we have withheld when we could have given it to the Lord's work or the less fortunate. Truly we are great sinners who need a great Savior!

If you see the truth of those two facts, as a result of the application of God's law to your heart, I encourage you to pray to him in this way right now:

Dear Lord, I know that I am more sinful and undeserving than I ever feared to admit. I do not love you with all my heart, soul, mind, and strength at all times, and I do not love others as much as I love myself. I ask you to forgive me in the name of Jesus and change my life so that I live for him instead of myself. And I thank you that although I am more sinful and undeserving than I ever feared to admit, in Christ I can be more loved and accepted than I ever dared to hope!

Once you know you have a relationship with Jesus Christ through repentance and faith, the Golden Rule becomes a key to your spiritual growth and service for others. The principles surrounding it in the passage above can be practiced by the power of the Holy Spirit working in you. You can be kind and merciful to those who don't deserve it. You can give freely without expecting anything in return. You can withhold judgment and believe the best about others, forgiving them from your heart because God has forgiven you so much more. And as you do, remember the final words in the Luke passage, where the Master Teacher concludes with an ironic and absolutely brilliant twist on the Golden Rule itself: "Give, and it will be given to you. Good measure, pressed down, shaken together, running over, will be put into your lap. For with the measure you use it will be measured back to you" (v. 38).

If we commit ourselves to treat others as we would like to be treated, we will find ourselves treated well by God and others—not by everyone, of course, but we will be blessed by many. Those who live by the Golden Rule are like a man who is freezing in the snow and who comes upon a fellow traveler in a worse condition than himself. He puts forth every effort to save him and is rewarded not only by the survival of the other man—now his grateful friend forever—but also by new warmth and life in his own freezing limbs. By helping the other person, he received great blessing as well.[59]

As I said at the beginning of this book and I hope you have seen along the way, the Golden Rule is a life-changing heavenly truth that will be worth far more to you than any earthly treasure, if you understand it rightly and practice it biblically. When rediscovered, this lost key to relationships will unlock the kind of supernatural power that can transform individual lives, the church, and the rest of society.

Endnotes

1. Jeffrey Wattles, *The Golden Rule* (New York: Oxford University Press, 1996), p. *v*.

2. In Eleanor Scott Meyers (ed.), *Envisioning the New City: A Reader on Urban Ministry* (Louisville, KY: Westminster/John Knox Press, 1992), pp. 90–91.

3. Quoted in Stephanie Condon, "Obama: I'm a 'Christian By Choice'", *CBSNews.com*, 28 September 2010.

4. Quoted in Jerry Adler, "'The Secret': Does Self-Help Book Really Help?", *Newsweek* (Culture section), 3 April 2007.

5. Matthew 22:40 is similar but talks about the two great commandments (love the Lord and love your neighbor) *depending on* the Law and the Prophets, whereas Matthew 7:12 speaks of the Golden Rule being *equivalent to* the Law and the Prophets. Matthew 22:40 speaks of basis or purpose, while 7:12 speaks of identity. The first is like saying "The speed limit is so we won't cause accidents" (the basis or purpose for the law), while the second is like saying "The speed limit is 55" (identity). However, despite the grammatical distinction between the two statements, I do think they have the same basic meaning. Jesus wanted people to know that the Golden Rule and the two great commandments both serve as summaries of the law, and also provide the basis or reason for the law (what it is intended to accomplish).

6. The commands of God include responsibilities to God as well as to each other (see Matt. 22:40 again), whereas the Golden Rule only refers to our relationships with other people. But we could say that by implication the rule *includes* how we relate to God, because we know from Scripture that we should love others *because* we love God, and such love for others is only meaningful when it flows from our love for God.

7. Most theological traditions list the first use of the law as the *pedagogical* use (teaching us our need for Christ), but the order of the other two have varied. Lutherans usually have placed the *didactic* use (teaching Christians how to live) second and the *civil* use (restraining evil in society) third, while the Reformed tradition (following John Calvin) normally has it the other way around. For what it's worth, my thoughts are that the pedagogical use is definitely the first, because Paul emphasizes that in his epistles so clearly, especially in Romans 3:19-20 and Galatians 3:19-24. (Those references even match each other…we must be meant to memorize them!) Also, I would suggest that the didactic is of second importance, because any real societal change would have to flow from individuals becoming more godly in their personal lives (not to mention the notorious philosophical, ethical, and practical difficulties of applying the Mosaic Law to societies other than ancient Israel). By the way, some theologians have questioned whether the didactic use of the law is biblical at all, saying that the New Testament does not mention it. But that view assumes a narrow definition of "the law" as only referring to the Mosaic Law, and then assumes that the Mosaic Law has no relation to the Christian. One passage among many that refutes

those assumptions would be James 1:22-25, where James talks about being doers of the Word and not hearers only, then refers to the Word as "the perfect law of liberty." Surely he meant all of the Scriptures, both Old and New Testaments, when he mentioned "the law" there.

8. Quoted in Marnie Jones, *Holy Toledo* (Lexington, KY: The University Press of Kentucky, 1998), p. 238.

9. *Webster's New World Dictionary*, Student Edition (New York: Simon & Schuster, Inc., 1981).

10. Wattles, p. 4.

11. Wattles, p. 5. The quotes from Paul Tillich are from his book, *The New Being*, (London: SCM Press, 1956), pp. 30–32.

12. Wattles, p. 6. The Shaw quote is taken from George Bernard Shaw, "Appendix", *Man and Superman* (Edinburgh, Scotland: Archibald Constable & Co., 1903), p. 227.

13. This story was attributed to Dr. William Willis in a circular email.

14. Peter J. Frederick, *Knights of the Golden Rule: The Intellectual as Christian Social Reformer in the 1890s* (Lexington, KY: The University Press of Kentucky, 1976), pp. 246–248.

15. Jeffrey Wattles, *The Golden Rule* (Oxford: Oxford University Press, 1996) and Harry J. Gensler, *Ethics and the Golden Rule* (Abingdon: Routledge, 2013).

16. Historian Gary Scott Smith explains this trend well in his book *The Search for Social Salvation: Social Christianity and America, 1880–1925* (Lanham, MD: Lexington Books, 2000): "As long as social service was viewed primarily as a way of loving and helping people, as an integral part of the attempt to apply biblical values to all areas of life, and little attention was paid to the theological foundation for these activities, a broad spectrum of American Protestants enthusiastically supported efforts to reform society during the optimistic Progressive era.... But after the movement ended, many professors and pastors increased their efforts to nail social activism to a foundation based more explicitly on liberal theology. This drove a deeper wedge between evangelicals and liberals who already disagreed over the authority and interpretation of the Bible. (pp. 349–350) The leadership of the movement passed in the early 1920s to Shailer Matthews, Harry Emerson Fosdick, and Harry Ward. Their more overt commitment to liberal theology and more radical stance on social issues helped push conservatives away from social Christianity" (pp. 384–385).

17. Frederick, p. 257.

18. "Socialism," first definition, *Webster's Dictionary*.

19. Frederick, p. 149.

20. Smith, p. 377.

21. Smith, p. 384.

22. Smith, quote from I. M. Haldeman, *The Mission of the Church in the World* (New York: Book Stall, 1917), p. 4 (italics in the original).

23. I realize this is not what most dispensationalists believe today (I have many

godly friends of that persuasion) — the beliefs of dispensationalists have evolved since those early years. But this was indeed a common perspective among its founders.

24. The few times I remember hearing about the Golden Rule during my childhood and youth, during which time I attended a dispensational "fundamentalist" church, left me with the impression that it was something *other people* believed in and valued, people who had the wrong theology. I realize that this is merely a hazy memory and impression from long ago, but it may not be far from the truth. To be fair, however, I must also add that one reviewer of this book said that he never heard anyone talk about the Golden Rule through many years of being a part of non-dispensational churches. So the neglect of the Golden Rule may well be universal among many kinds of denominations.

25. The different camps have had varying understandings of the term "literal interpretation," of course. Non-dispensationalist conservatives believe that the natural or "literal" reading of prophecy allows for figurative or typological meanings, and that such interpretations are consistent with a strong belief in the inerrancy of Scripture. The first and last prophecies in the Old Testament, for example, both clearly contain figurative elements (Gen. 3:15 and Mal. 4:5). So I believe it is a mistake to associate any millennial view with theological liberalism — they have all been held by true believers throughout church history.

26. Despite my high regard and respect for the lives and work of many who believe this, I don't think it can be proven from Scripture (or supported by experience) that the world must only get worse until Christ returns. Even if the Bible teaches that the times just before Christ's return will be bad, how do we know that those particular bad times have arrived — in other words, how can we ever know that any current bad times won't be followed by good times? The history of the church has been a cycle of good and bad times — not a one-direction decline. It has seen an ebb and flow that has included significant revivals, such as the Reformation in Europe and the Great Awakenings in America. Couldn't we see another revival, even a worldwide one, sometime before the Lord returns? Also, the idea that everything is getting worse and cannot turn around also seems rather provincial — based on Americans looking just at American culture. What about the masses of people coming to Christ in other countries? Consider, for example, China, the world's largest country, and the effects that a great movement of God is having on that culture. The United States may seem to be declining spiritually, but that may not be true for other places around the globe. For Christians to give up on trying to "make the world a better place" through the practice of biblical principles like the Golden Rule seems short-sighted to me. Couldn't it become a self-fulfilling prophecy? Believing that the world will just get worse, Christians give up trying to make it better, and the resulting lack of effort ensures that it gets worse!

27. Gary Scott Smith explains this well in his book *The Search for Social Salvation:* "Conservatives claimed that some proponents of social Christianity made improving society more important than saving souls; they substituted social reconstruction for personal salvation. This approach, conservatives

protested, would inevitably weaken concern for both individual salvation and sound doctrine. It could lead people to conclude... that the Christianization of society was the entire message of the gospel. Greene complained that many Social Gospelers considered social service "the essence of Christianity rather than one of its fruits" and made social amelioration rather than the preaching of the gospel the primary task of the church." p. 371, quote is from William B. Greene Jr., *Princeton Theological Review* 10 (April 1912), p. 360.

28. *Ibid,* quote from A. C. Gaebelein, "The Crime Waves," *Our Hope* 27 (March 1921), pp. 547–548.

29. *Ibid*, p. 372.

30. *Ibid*, p. 305, quote from Rolf Lunden, *Business and Religion in the American 1920s* (Westport, CT: Greenwood Press, 1988), p. 152.

31. Frederick, p. 180.

32. *Ibid*, p. 182.

33. J. Gresham Machen, *Christianity and Liberalism* (Grand Rapids, MI: Eerdmans, 1994), p. 38.

34. Wattles, pp. 73-74. The sermon on the Golden Rule that Wattles says may be Martin Luther's first sermon is found in *Luther's Works* (Philadelphia: Fortress Press, 1959), Volume 51, pp. 5-13.

35. Edward Gibbon, *Decline and Fall of the Roman Empire* (accessed 02/25/2021 at sacredtexts.org), Vol. 5, Chapter LIV, footnote 36.

36. Bruce Metzger, "The Designation 'The Golden Rule,'" in *Expository Times* 69, July 1958. The quote from Gibbon is a footnote near the close of Chapter 54. His vilification of Calvin, by the way, illustrates a superficial understanding of the Golden Rule. No doubt Calvin thought he was practicing the Golden Rule in the Servetus incident, and we could imagine his defense. "If the roles were reversed and I was dangerous heretic," the famous Reformer might have said, "I would have wanted to be punished in the same way, to bring me to repentance or at least eliminate a ruinous influence upon the church." Yes, Calvin had been threatened with the same fate by the Roman church, but if he was right in his theology, he would be vindicated in the same way an innocent man accused of murder could himself be acquitted but still support the death penalty for those who are truly guilty.

37. Wattles, *The Golden Rule,* p. 78.

38. Confucius, *Analects* 15.23, translated by Wing-tsit Chan.

39. Plato, *Laws* 913a, translated by A.E. Taylor in 1961, cited in Wattles, *The Golden Rule,* p. 35.

40. This quote from the Book of Tobit, and the following two quotes in this paragraph from the Dead Sea Scrolls and Rabbi Hillel, are all from Wattles, pp. 42–47.

41. Martin Luther, *Commentary on Galatians: Modern-English Edition* (Grand Rapids, MI: Fleming H. Revell, 1988), p. 94.

42. Dr. Tony Allesandra says this on his website at https://www.alessandra.

com/abouttony/aboutpr.asp (accessed 2/25/21): "We have all heard of the Golden Rule—and many people aspire to live by it. The Golden Rule is not a panacea. Think about it: 'Do unto others as you would have them do unto you.' The Golden Rule implies the basic assumption that other people would like to be treated the way that you would like to be treated. The alternative to the Golden Rule is the Platinum Rule: 'Treat others the way they want to be treated.' Ah hah! What a difference. The Platinum Rule accommodates the feelings of others. The focus of relationships shifts from 'this is what I want, so I'll give everyone the same thing' to 'let me first understand what they want and then I'll give it to them.'"

43. This is found in Kant's work *Grounding of the Metaphysics of Morals*, Kant 1983, p. 429.

44. Meyers, ed., pp. 90–94.

45. Wattles, p. 5. The Tillich quotes are from Tillich, *The New Being*, pp. 30–32.

46. *Ibid*, p. 6. The Shaw quote is taken from the appendix to *Man and Superman*.

47. *Ibid*, p. 83. No Clarke citation on this quote, but it is found in Clarke 1969, on or near pp. 207–209.

48. *Ibid*, emphasis his.

49. *Ibid*, emphasis his.

50. Charles Spurgeon, *Commentary on Matthew: The Gospel of the Kingdom*, accessed 2/25/21 at http://www.spurgeongems.org/chs_matthew.pdf.

51. Wattles, p. 9.

52. Although the text of the novel says that Scrooge went to church on that Christmas morning, that part is unfortunately left out of most movie and theater versions of the story.

53. I am not saying that everything taught or believed by people who use these slogans is necessarily true, but I do think an emphasis on God's free grace in Christ, justification by faith alone, and the role of faith in sanctification is very important for Christians to avoid problems like self-righteousness as well as depression from the guilt of our sins.

54. Spurgeon, *Commentary on Matthew*, accessed 2/25/21 at http://www.spurgeongems.org/chs_matthew.pdf.

55. Quoted in H. A. W. Meyer, *Commentary on Matthew*, 1864, public domain.

56. John Gill, *Exposition of the Entire Bible*, 1763, public domain.

57. H. A .W. Meyer, *Commentary on Matthew*, 1864, public domain.

58. For more about this, see Steve Corbett and Brian Fikkert, *When Helping Hurts* (Moody, 2014).

59. Adapted from *The Biblical Illustrator*, Electronic Database, Copyright © 2002, 2003, 2006, 2011 by Biblesoft, Inc.

Devoted
Great Men and Their Godly Moms

Tim Challies | 128 pages

Women shaped the men who changed the world.

bit.ly/devotedbook

Who Am I?
Identity in Christ

Jerry Bridges | 91 pages

Jerry Bridges unpacks Scripture to give the Christian eight clear, simple, interlocking answers to one of the most essential questions of life.

bit.ly/WHOAMI

The Company We Keep
In Search of Biblical Friendship

Jonathan Holmes
Foreword by Ed Welch | 112 pages

Biblical friendship is deep, honest, pure, tranparent, and liberating. It is also attainable.

bit.ly/B-Friend

The Ten Commandments of Progressive Christianity

Michael J. Kruger | 56 pages

A cautionary look at ten dangerously appealing half-truths.

bit.ly/TENCOM

Endorsed by Collin Hansen,
Kevin DeYoung, Michael Horton

Do More Better
A Practical Guide to Productivity

Tim Challies | 114 pages

Don't try to do it all. Do more good. Better.

bit.ly/domorebetter

The God of the Mundane: Reflections on Ordinary Life for Ordinary People

(second edition)

Matthew B. Redmond | 134 pages

It's OK to not be a "radical" Christian. Our life is not about what we do for God. It's about what he does for us.

bit.ly/MUNDANE

Don't miss these fully inductive Bible studies for women from Keri Folmar!

Loved by churches. Endorsed by Kristi Anyabwile, Connie Dever, Gloria Furman, Kathleen Nielson, and Diane Schreiner.

The series currently consists of six volumes.

10 weeks	*10 weeks*	*10 weeks*

Joy! (Philippians)	*Faith* (James)	*Grace* (Ephesians)

11 weeks	*11 weeks*	*9 weeks*

Son of God (Gospel of Mark, 2 volumes)   *Zeal* (Titus)

Servanthood as Worship
The Privilege of Life in a Local Church

Nate Palmer | 112 pages

Celebrating our calling to serve in the church, motivated by the grace that is ours in the gospel.

bit.ly/Srvnt

Run to Win:
The Lifelong Pursuits of a Godly Man

Tim Challies | 163 pages

Plan to run, train to run...run to win.

bit.ly/RUN2WIN

The Joy Project:
An Introduction to Calvinism
(with Study Guide)

Tony Reinke
Foreword by John Piper | 168 pages

True happiness isn't found. It finds you.

bit.ly/JOYPROJECT

Made in the USA
Columbia, SC
02 September 2022

66514998R00080